Hamburger
MAGIC
in Minutes

D1469259

Publications International, Ltd.

Favorite Brand Name Recipes at www.fbnr.com

Pictured on the front cover: Rapid Ragu® Chili *(page 136).*
Pictured on the back cover *(counterclockwise from top):* Hearty Nachos *(page 26),* Italian-Style Meat Loaf *(page 66)* and Heartland Shepherd's Pie *(page 92).*

Microwave Cooking: Microwave ovens vary in wattage. Use the cooking times as guidelines and check for doneness before adding more time.

Preparation/Cooking Times: Preparation times are based on the approximate amount of time required to assemble the recipe before cooking, baking, chilling or serving. These times include preparation steps such as measuring, chopping and mixing. The fact that some preparations and cooking can be done simultaneously is taken into account. Preparation of optional ingredients and serving suggestions is not included.

Contents

p. 11

p. 67

p. 131

Sensational

Starters

Bite Size Tacos

1 pound ground beef
1 package (1.25 ounces) taco seasoning mix
2 cups *French's*® French Fried Onions
¼ cup chopped fresh cilantro
32 bite-size round tortilla chips
¾ cup sour cream
1 cup shredded Cheddar cheese

1. Cook beef in nonstick skillet over medium-high heat 5 minutes or until browned; drain. Stir in taco seasoning mix, *¾ cup water, 1 cup* French Fried Onions and cilantro. Simmer 5 minutes or until flavors are blended, stirring often.

2. Preheat oven to 350°F. Arrange tortilla chips on foil-lined baking sheet. Top with beef mixture, sour cream, remaining *1 cup* onions and cheese.

3. Bake 5 minutes or until cheese is melted and onions are golden.   *Makes 8 appetizer servings*

Prep Time: 5 minutes
Cook Time: 15 minutes

Crispy Oriental Wontons

½ pound ground pork

1 cup VELVEETA® Mild Cheddar Shredded Pasteurized Process Cheese Food

2 tablespoons green onion slices

1 teaspoon minced peeled gingerroot

1 teaspoon sesame oil (optional)

32 wonton wrappers

Sesame seeds

Dipping Sauce (recipe follows)

• Preheat oven to 425°F.

• Brown meat; drain. Mix together meat, Velveeta, onion, gingerroot and sesame oil.

• For each wonton, place scant tablespoonful meat mixture in center of one wonton wrapper. Bring corners together over meat mixture; twist and pinch together, enclosing meat mixture in dough. Flatten bottom slightly. Place on cookie sheet. Brush lightly with water; sprinkle with sesame seeds.

• Bake 10 to 12 minutes or until golden brown. Serve warm with Dipping Sauce.   *Makes 32 appetizers*

Prep Time: 25 minutes
Cook Time: 12 minutes

Dipping Sauce

2 tablespoons soy sauce

1 tablespoon cold water

1 tablespoon rice wine (optional)

• Mix together ingredients until blended.

Makes ¼ cup

Crispy Oriental Wontons

Mini Burgers

1 pound ground chicken

¼ cup Italian-style dry
bread crumbs

¼ cup chili sauce

1 egg white

1 tablespoon white
Worcestershire sauce

2 teaspoons Dijon-style
mustard

½ teaspoon dried thyme
leaves

¼ teaspoon garlic powder

32 thin slices plum tomatoes
(about 3 medium)

½ cup sweet onion slices
(about 1 small)

16 slices cocktail rye or
pumpernickel bread

Mustard (optional)

Pickle slices (optional)

Snipped chives or green
onion tops (optional)

1. Preheat oven to 350°F. Combine chicken, bread crumbs, chili sauce, egg white, Worcestershire sauce, mustard, thyme and garlic powder in medium bowl. Form mixture into 16 patties.

2. Place patties in 15×10-inch jelly-roll pan. Bake, uncovered, 10 to 15 minutes or until patties are no longer pink in centers.

3. Place 2 tomato slices and 1 onion slice on each bread slice. Top each with 1 patty; add dollops of mustard, pickle slices and chives, if desired.

Makes 16 servings

Spicy Beef Turnovers

½ **pound lean ground beef or turkey**

2 **cloves garlic, minced**

2 **tablespoons soy sauce**

1 **tablespoon water**

½ **teaspoon cornstarch**

1 **teaspoon curry powder**

¼ **teaspoon Chinese five-spice powder**

¼ **teaspoon red pepper flakes**

2 **tablespoons minced green onion**

1 **package (7.5 ounces) refrigerated biscuits**

1 **egg**

1 **tablespoon water**

1. Preheat oven to 400°F. Cook beef with garlic in medium skillet over medium-high heat until beef is no longer pink, stirring to separate. Spoon off fat.

2. Blend soy sauce and 1 tablespoon water into cornstarch in cup until smooth. Add soy sauce mixture, curry powder, five-spice powder and red pepper flakes to skillet. Cook and stir 30 seconds or until liquid is absorbed, stirring constantly. Remove from heat; stir in onion.

3. Roll each biscuit between 2 sheets of waxed paper into 4-inch rounds. Spoon heaping 1 tablespoon beef mixture onto one side of each biscuit; fold over, forming a semi-circle. Pinch edges together to seal.*

4. Arrange turnovers on baking sheet coated with nonstick cooking spray. Beat egg with 1 tablespoon water in cup; brush lightly over turnovers. Bake 9 to 10 minutes or until golden brown. Serve warm or at room temperature. *Makes 10 appetizers*

*At this point, turnovers may be wrapped and frozen up to 3 months. Thaw completely before proceeding as directed in step 4.

Sensational Starters

Thai Lamb & Couscous Rolls

16 large napa or Chinese cabbage leaves, stems trimmed

2 tablespoons minced fresh ginger

1 teaspoon red pepper flakes

⅔ cup uncooked quick-cooking couscous

½ pound ground lean lamb

½ cup chopped green onions

3 cloves garlic, minced

¼ cup plus 2 tablespoons minced fresh cilantro or mint, divided

2 tablespoons reduced-sodium soy sauce

1 tablespoon lime juice

1 teaspoon dark sesame oil

1 cup plain nonfat yogurt

1. Place 4 cups water in medium saucepan; bring to a boil over high heat. Drop cabbage leaves into water; cook 30 seconds; drain. Rinse under cold water until cool; pat dry with paper towels.

2. Place 1 cup water, ginger and red pepper flakes in medium saucepan; bring to a boil over high heat. Stir in couscous; cover. Remove saucepan from heat; let stand 5 minutes.

3. Spray large saucepan with nonstick cooking spray; add lamb, onions and garlic. Cook and stir over medium-high heat 5 minutes or until lamb is no longer pink. Remove lamb from skillet; drain in colander.

4. Combine couscous, lamb, ¼ cup cilantro, soy sauce, lime juice and oil in medium bowl. Spoon evenly down centers of cabbage leaves. Fold ends of cabbage leaves over filling; roll up. Combine yogurt and remaining 2 tablespoons cilantro in small bowl; spoon evenly over rolls. Serve warm. Garnish as desired.

Makes 16 appetizers

Thai Lamb & Couscous Rolls

Savory Beef Swirls

½ pound lean ground beef

⅓ cup shredded Cheddar cheese (about 1 ½ ounces)

¼ cup A.1.® Original or A.1.® BOLD & SPICY Steak Sauce

¼ cup chopped red bell pepper

2 tablespoons chopped green onion

1 (8-ounce) can refrigerated crescent dinner rolls

Mix ground beef, cheese, steak sauce, pepper and green onion; set aside.

Separate dough into 4 rectangles; press perforations to seal. Divide and spread reserved beef mixture on each rectangle. Roll up rectangles from long edges; press dough together to seal. Cut each roll crosswise into 8 pieces; place pieces, cut sides down, on ungreased baking sheets.

Bake at 375°F 12 to 15 minutes or until golden brown. Serve immediately. Garnish as desired.

Makes 32 appetizers

Savory Beef Swirls

Cheesy Quesadillas

½ **pound ground beef**

1 **medium onion, chopped**

¼ **teaspoon salt**

1 **can (4.5 ounces) chopped green chilies, drained**

1 **jar (26 to 28 ounces) RAGÚ® Robusto!™ Pasta Sauce, divided**

8 **(6½-inch) flour tortillas**

1 **tablespoon olive or vegetable oil**

2 **cups shredded Cheddar and/or mozzarella cheese (about 8 ounces)**

1. Preheat oven to 400°F. In 12-inch skillet, brown ground beef with onion and salt over medium-high heat; drain. Stir in chilies and ½ cup Ragú Pasta Sauce; set aside.

2. Meanwhile, evenly brush one side of 4 tortillas with half of oil. On cookie sheets, arrange tortillas, oil-sides down. Evenly top with ½ of cheese, beef filling, then remaining cheese. Top with remaining 4 tortillas, then brush tops with remaining oil.

3. Bake 10 minutes or until cheese is melted. To serve, cut each quesadilla into 4 wedges. Serve with remaining sauce, heated. Garnish as desired.   *Makes 4 servings*

Prep Time: 10 minutes
Cook Time: 15 minutes

Cheesy Quesadillas

Swedish-Style Meatballs

4 tablespoons butter or margarine, divided

1 cup minced onion

1 pound lean ground beef

½ pound lean ground veal

½ pound lean ground pork

1 cup fresh bread crumbs

2 eggs, slightly beaten

½ teaspoon salt

¼ teaspoon black pepper

⅛ teaspoon grated nutmeg

3 tablespoons all-purpose flour

1¼ cups milk

¼ cup half-and-half

1 egg yolk

½ teaspoon salt

Melt 2 tablespoons butter in large skillet over medium heat. Add onion. Cook and stir 8 to 10 minutes or until very soft. Remove from heat and set aside. Combine beef, veal, pork, bread crumbs, beaten eggs, salt, pepper and nutmeg in large bowl. Add onion mixture; mix well. Shape into balls (use 2 tablespoons meat mixture for dinner-sized meatball or 1 tablespoon for cocktail-sized). Set aside.

Preheat oven to 200°F.

Reheat skillet over medium heat. Add ¼ to ⅓ of meatballs. *Do not crowd pan.* Cook 8 minutes, shaking pan to allow meatballs to roll and brown evenly. Reduce heat to medium-low. Cook 15 to 20 minutes or until cooked through. Transfer to covered casserole dish and keep warm in oven.

Meanwhile, wipe out skillet. Melt remaining 2 tablespoons butter over medium heat. Whisk in flour. Stir well. Combine milk, half-and-half, egg yolk and salt in small bowl. Slowly stir into flour mixture. Reduce heat to medium-low. Cook and stir 3 minutes or until thickened. Remove dish from oven and pour sauce over meatballs. Serve immediately.

Makes 36 dinner-sized meatballs or 72 cocktail-sized meatballs

Swedish-Style Meatballs

Spring Rolls

½ **pound ground pork**

1 **teaspoon KIKKOMAN®**
   Soy Sauce

1 **teaspoon dry sherry**

½ **teaspoon garlic salt**

2 **tablespoons vegetable oil**

3 **cups fresh bean sprouts**

½ **cup sliced onion**

1 **tablespoon KIKKOMAN®**
   Soy Sauce

1 **tablespoon cornstarch**

¾ **cup water, divided**

8 **egg roll wrappers**

½ **cup quick biscuit mix**

1 **egg, beaten**
   Vegetable oil for frying
   Hot mustard, tomato
      ketchup and
      KIKKOMAN® Soy Sauce

Combine pork, 1 teaspoon soy sauce, sherry and garlic salt; mix well. Let stand 15 minutes. Heat 2 tablespoons oil in hot wok or large skillet over medium-high heat; brown pork mixture in hot oil. Add bean sprouts, onion and 1 tablespoon soy sauce. Stir-fry until vegetables are tender-crisp; drain and cool. Dissolve cornstarch in ¼ cup water. Place about ⅓ cup pork mixture on lower half of egg roll wrapper. Moisten left and right edges with cornstarch mixture. Fold bottom edge up just to cover filling. Fold left and right edges ½ inch over; roll jelly-roll fashion. Moisten top edge with cornstarch mixture and seal. Complete all rolls. Combine biscuit mix, egg and remaining ½ cup water in small bowl; dip each roll in batter. Heat oil for frying in wok or large saucepan over medium-high heat to 370°F. Deep-fry rolls, a few at a time, in hot oil 5 to 7 minutes, or until golden brown, turning often. Drain on paper towels. Slice each roll in half. Serve with mustard, ketchup and soy sauce as desired.   *Makes 8 appetizer servings*

Spring Rolls

Pork Empanaditas (Mini Turnovers)

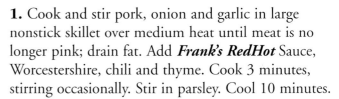

¾ pound ground pork
1 small onion, finely
    chopped
2 cloves garlic, crushed
3 tablespoons *Frank's*®
    RedHot® Cayenne
    Pepper Sauce
1 tablespoon *French's*®
    Worcestershire Sauce
2 teaspoons chili powder
½ teaspoon ground thyme
½ cup chopped fresh
    parsley
2 refrigerated pie crust
    sheets (9 inches)
1 egg plus 2 tablespoons
    water, beaten
    Sesame seeds

1. Cook and stir pork, onion and garlic in large nonstick skillet over medium heat until meat is no longer pink; drain fat. Add *Frank's RedHot* Sauce, Worcestershire, chili and thyme. Cook 3 minutes, stirring occasionally. Stir in parsley. Cool 10 minutes.

2. Preheat oven to 375°F. Line baking sheets with foil; grease foil. Roll each pie crust sheet into 13-inch circle on lightly floured surface. Cut into rounds using a 4-inch cookie cutter.* Brush edges of each round with egg mixture. Spoon 1 tablespoon pork mixture into center of each round. Fold rounds in half, pressing edges to seal.

3. Place filled rounds onto baking sheets. Prick tops with fork; brush lightly with remaining egg mixture. Sprinkle with sesame seeds. Re-roll pastry scraps; cut and fill with remaining pork mixture.

4. Bake 20 minutes or until golden. Serve warm.

Makes about 1½ dozen empanaditas

*Or, use an empty 28-ounce can for 4-inch cookie cutter.

Prep Time: 30 minutes
Bake Time: 20 minutes

Sweet & Sour Cocktail Meatballs

1 pound ground turkey

¾ cup plain dry bread
    crumbs

½ cup GREY POUPON®
    Dijon Mustard, divided

½ cup chopped green
    onions, divided

1 egg, beaten

½ teaspoon ground ginger

½ teaspoon ground black
    pepper

1 (8-ounce) can pineapple
    chunks, undrained

⅓ cup firmly packed light
    brown sugar

¼ cup apple cider vinegar

¼ cup diced red bell
    pepper

1 teaspoon cornstarch

Combine turkey, bread crumbs, ¼ cup mustard, ¼ cup green onions, egg, ginger and black pepper in large bowl. Shape into 32 (1-inch) balls. Place in greased 13×9×2-inch baking pan. Bake at 350°F for 20 minutes. Remove from oven and set aside.

Combine pineapple chunks with juice, sugar, vinegar, red bell pepper, cornstarch and remaining ¼ cup mustard and green onions in medium saucepan. Cook over medium heat until sauce thickens and begins to boil. Spoon pineapple sauce over meatballs. Bake 5 to 7 minutes more or until meatballs are done. Spoon into serving dish and serve with toothpicks.

Makes 32 appetizers

Magical Tip

Ground turkey's low-fat content and excellent flavor make it a popular replacement for ground beef in a wide variety of recipes.

Pizza Snack Cups

1 can (12 ounces)
   refrigerated biscuits
   (10 biscuits)
½ pound ground beef
1 jar (14 ounces) RAGÚ®
   Pizza Quick® Sauce
½ cup shredded mozzarella
   cheese (about
   2 ounces)

1. Preheat oven to 375°F. In 12-cup muffin pan, evenly press each biscuit onto bottom and up side of cup, lining 10 cups in all; chill until ready to fill.

2. In 10-inch skillet, brown ground beef over medium-high heat; drain. Stir in Ragú Pizza Quick Sauce and heat through.

3. Evenly spoon beef mixture into prepared muffin cups. Bake 15 minutes. Sprinkle with cheese and bake an additional 5 minutes or until cheese is melted and biscuits are golden. Let stand 5 minutes. Gently remove pizza cups from muffin pan and serve.

Makes 10 pizza cups

Prep Time: 10 minutes
Cook Time: 25 minutes

Pizza Snack Cups

Jamaican Meat Patties

1 pound ground beef

1 onion, chopped

1 clove garlic, minced

¼ cup *Frank's® RedHot®* Cayenne Pepper Sauce

2¼ teaspoons curry powder, divided

1 teaspoon dried thyme leaves

1 egg, beaten

2 sheets folded refrigerated unbaked pie crusts (15 ounce package)

1. Cook beef, onion and garlic in nonstick skillet 5 minutes or until meat is browned, stirring to separate meat. Drain fat. Stir in **Frank's RedHot** Sauce, *½ cup water, 2 teaspoons* curry powder and thyme. Cook 5 minutes or until liquid is evaporated, stirring often. Cool slightly. Mix egg with *1 tablespoon water* and remaining *¼ teaspoon* curry powder; set aside.

2. Preheat oven to 400°F. Roll out each pie crust sheet into slightly larger round on lightly floured board. Cut out 10 rounds using 5-inch cookie cutter, re-rolling scraps as necessary. Brush edges of rounds with some of egg mixture. Spoon about 3 tablespoons cooled meat mixture in center of each round. Fold rounds in half, pressing edges with floured fork to seal.

3. Place patties onto lightly greased baking sheets. Brush tops with remaining egg mixture. Bake 15 minutes or until crusts are crisp.

Makes 10 patties

Tip: A small bowl measuring 5 inches across may be used for the cookie cutter. Patties can be prepared ahead, wrapped securely and frozen before baking. Bake, uncovered, at 400°F for 15 minutes. To make party-size appetizers, use a 3-inch round cutter.

Prep Time: 15 minutes
Cook Time: 25 minutes

Beefy Guacamole Dip

1 pound ground beef
1 large onion, minced
1 package (1.0 ounce) LAWRY'S® Taco Spices & Seasonings
¾ cup water
1½ cups guacamole
2 medium tomatoes, chopped
1 cup (4 ounces) shredded cheddar cheese
Tortilla chips

In large skillet, cook ground beef and onion over medium-high heat until beef is browned and crumbly; drain fat. Add Taco Spices & Seasonings and water; mix well. Bring to a boil over medium-high heat; reduce heat to low and simmer, uncovered, 10 minutes or until liquid is absorbed. In small bowl, combine guacamole and tomatoes; mix well. In large bowl, layer half of beef mixture, guacamole and cheese; repeat layers.

Makes about 4 cups

Serving Suggestion: Serve immediately with tortilla chips.

Beefy Stuffed Mushrooms

1 pound lean ground beef
2 teaspoons prepared horseradish
1 teaspoon chopped chives
1 clove garlic, minced
¼ teaspoon black pepper
18 large mushrooms
⅔ cup dry white wine

1. Thoroughly mix ground beef, horseradish, chives, garlic and pepper in medium bowl.

2. Remove stems from mushrooms; discard stems. Stuff mushroom caps with beef mixture.

3. Place stuffed mushrooms in shallow baking dish; pour wine over mushrooms. Bake in preheated 350°F oven until meat is browned, about 20 minutes.

Makes 1½ dozen

Hearty Nachos

Sensational Starters

1 pound ground beef

1 envelope LIPTON® RECIPE SECRETS® Onion Soup Mix

1 can (19 ounces) black beans, rinsed and drained

1 cup prepared salsa

1 package (8½ ounces) plain tortilla chips

1 cup shredded Cheddar cheese (about 4 ounces)

1. In 12-inch nonstick skillet, brown ground beef over medium-high heat; drain.

2. Stir in soup mix, black beans and salsa. Bring to a boil over high heat. Reduce heat to low and simmer 5 minutes or until heated through.

3. Arrange tortilla chips on serving platter. Spread beef mixture over chips; sprinkle with Cheddar cheese. Top, if desired, with sliced green onions, sliced pitted ripe olives, chopped tomato and chopped cilantro.

Makes 8 servings

Prep Time: 10 minutes
Cook Time: 12 minutes

Sombrero Taco Cups

1 pound ground beef or pork

1 package (1.0 ounce) LAWRY'S® Taco Spices & Seasonings

¾ cup water

¼ cup salsa

2 cans (8 ounces each) refrigerated biscuits

½ cup (2 ounces) grated cheddar cheese

In medium skillet, cook ground beef until browned and crumbly; drain fat. Add Taco Spices & Seasonings and water; mix well. Bring to a boil over medium-high heat; reduce heat to low and simmer, uncovered, 10 minutes. Stir in salsa. Separate biscuits and press each biscuit into an ungreased muffin cup. Spoon equal amounts of meat mixture into each muffin cup; sprinkle each with cheese. Bake, uncovered, in 350°F oven 12 minutes or until biscuit cups are browned and cheese is melted.

Makes 12 cups

Serving Suggestion: Serve as a main dish or as a snack.

Hint: For an extra treat, flatten any leftover biscuit dough into disks; sprinkle with cinnamon-sugar mixture and bake in 350°F oven 5 to 7 minutes or until golden.

Hearty Nachos

Empandillas

½ pound ground beef

1 cup chopped black olives

¾ cup chopped fresh
   mushrooms

¼ cup water

1 package (1.0 ounce)
   LAWRY'S® Taco Spices
   & Seasonings

2 cans (8 ounces each)
   refrigerated crescent
   rolls

1 egg white, beaten

In medium bowl, combine ground beef, olives, mushrooms, water and Taco Spices & Seasonings; mix well. Roll out crescent roll dough into 12-inch squares. Cut each sheet into 9 squares. Place approximately 2 teaspoons meat mixture in center of each square; moisten edges with water. Fold one corner over to form triangle and pinch edges together to seal. Brush with egg white. Place on ungreased baking sheet. Bake in 375°F oven 15 to 20 minutes or until golden brown.

Makes 18 appetizers

Serving Suggestion: Serve with guacamole and sour cream.

Hint: Stir 3 tablespoons grated cheese into filling for extra flavor.

Crunchy Mexican Turkey Tidbits

1 pound ground turkey

1 egg, beaten

2 garlic cloves, minced

¼ cup *each* finely chopped
   onion and dry bread
   crumbs

1 teaspoon chili powder

½ teaspoon cumin

4 ounces tortilla chips,
   finely crushed

   Nonstick cooking spray

¾ cup nonfat sour cream

½ cup salsa

1. In medium bowl combine turkey, egg, garlic, onion, bread crumbs, chili powder and cumin; shape into approximately 36 (¾-inch) balls.

2. Place crushed chips on plate. Roll each meatball in chips, coating thoroughly. On 15×10×1-inch baking pan lightly coated with nonstick cooking spray, arrange meatballs. Bake at 350°F 20 minutes or until meat is no longer pink in center.

3. In small bowl combine sour cream and salsa. Use as dip for meatballs.

Makes 36 meatballs

*Favorite recipe from **National Turkey Federation***

Egg Rolls

¼ cup soy sauce

2 tablespoons dry sherry

4 teaspoons cornstarch

Peanut or vegetable oil

6 cups chopped or shredded cabbage or preshredded coleslaw mix or cabbage (about 12 ounces)

1 cup chopped mushrooms

⅔ cup thinly sliced green onions

½ pound ground beef, pork or turkey

3 cloves garlic, minced

¼ teaspoon red pepper flakes

12 egg roll wrappers *or* 64 wonton wrappers

Sweet and sour sauce for dipping

Chinese hot mustard (optional)

1. Blend soy sauce and sherry into cornstarch in cup until smooth.

2. Heat wok or large skillet over medium-high heat. Add 1 tablespoon oil; heat until hot. Add cabbage, mushrooms and green onions; stir-fry 2 minutes (cabbage will still be crisp). Remove; set aside.

3. Add beef, garlic and red pepper flakes to wok; cook until beef is no longer pink, stirring to separate. Spoon off fat.

4. Stir soy sauce mixture and add to wok. Stir-fry 2 minutes or until sauce boils and thickens. Return cabbage mixture to wok; heat through, mixing well.*

5. Place each egg roll wrapper with one point toward edge of counter. Spoon filling across and just below center of wrapper; use heaping ⅓ cup filling for each egg roll wrapper or 1 tablespoon filling for each wonton wrapper.

6. To form egg roll, fold bottom point of wrapper up over filling. Fold side points over filling, forming an envelope shape. Moisten inside edges of top point with water and roll egg roll toward that point, pressing firmly to seal. Repeat with remaining wrappers and filling.

7. Pour ½ inch oil into large skillet. Heat oil to 375°F. Fry egg rolls, 2 or 3 at a time, or mini-egg rolls, 6 to 8 at time, 2 minutes per side or until crisp and golden brown. Drain on paper towels. Serve with sweet and sour sauce and hot mustard, if desired.

Makes about 12 egg rolls or 64 mini egg rolls

*Egg roll filling may be made ahead to this point; cover and refrigerate up to 24 hours. When ready to use, heat mixture until hot. Proceed as directed in step 5.

Sensational **Starters**

Quintessential Quickies

Dijon Bacon Cheeseburgers

1 cup shredded Cheddar cheese (4 ounces)

5 tablespoons GREY POUPON® Dijon Mustard, divided

2 teaspoons dried minced onion

1 teaspoon prepared horseradish

1 pound lean ground beef

4 onion sandwich rolls, split and toasted

1 cup shredded lettuce

4 slices tomato

4 slices bacon, cooked and halved

In small bowl, combine cheese, 3 tablespoons mustard, onion and horseradish; set aside.

In medium bowl, combine ground beef and remaining 2 tablespoons mustard; shape mixture into 4 patties. Grill or broil burgers over medium heat for 5 minutes on each side or until desired doneness; top with cheese mixture and cook until cheese melts, about 2 minutes. Top each roll bottom with ¼ cup shredded lettuce, 1 tomato slice, burger, 2 bacon pieces and roll top. Serve immediately. *Makes 4 burgers*

Dijon Bacon Cheeseburger

America's Favorite Cheddar Beef Burgers

1 pound ground beef

⅓ cup A.1.® Steak Sauce, divided

1 medium onion, cut into strips

1 medium green or red bell pepper, cut into strips

1 tablespoon margarine or butter

4 ounces Cheddar cheese, sliced

4 hamburger rolls

4 tomato slices

Mix ground beef and 3 tablespoons steak sauce; shape mixture into 4 burgers. Set aside.

Cook and stir onion and pepper in margarine or butter in medium skillet until tender. Stir in remaining steak sauce; keep warm.

Grill burgers over medium heat for 4 minutes on each side or until done. When almost done, top with cheese; grill until cheese melts. Spoon 2 tablespoons onion mixture onto each roll bottom; top each with burger, tomato slice, remaining onion mixture and roll top. Serve immediately. *Makes 4 servings*

America's Favorite Cheddar Beef Burger

Original Ortega® Taco Recipe

1 pound ground beef

¾ cup water

1 package (1¼ ounces)
ORTEGA® Taco
Seasoning Mix

1 package (12) ORTEGA®
Taco Shells, warmed

Toppings: shredded
lettuce, chopped
tomatoes, shredded
mild Cheddar cheese,
ORTEGA® Thick &
Smooth Taco Sauce

BROWN beef; drain. Stir in water and seasoning mix. Bring to a boil. Reduce heat to low; cook, stirring occasionally, for 5 to 6 minutes or until mixture is thickened.

FILL taco shells with beef mixture. Top with lettuce, tomatoes, cheese and taco sauce.   *Makes 6 servings*

Parmesan Burgers

1 pound ground beef

⅓ cup A.1.® Steak Sauce,
divided

2 tablespoons grated
Parmesan cheese

½ cup prepared spaghetti
sauce

4 mozzarella cheese slices
(about 2 ounces)

4 English muffins, split and
grilled or toasted

Mix ground beef, 3 tablespoons steak sauce and Parmesan cheese in small bowl; shape mixture into 4 patties. Set aside.

Blend remaining steak sauce and spaghetti sauce in small bowl; set aside.

Grill burgers over medium heat for 4 minutes on each side or until done. When almost done, top each with mozzarella cheese; grill until cheese melts. Spread 1 tablespoon steak sauce mixture on each muffin bottom; top each with burger, remaining sauce and muffin top. Serve immediately.   *Makes 4 servings*

Original Ortega® Taco Recipe

Big D Ranch Burgers

1 cup sliced onion

⅓ cup green bell pepper strips

⅓ cup red bell pepper strips

1 tablespoon margarine or butter

3 tablespoons A.1.® Steak Sauce

2 teaspoons prepared horseradish

1 pound ground beef

4 onion rolls, split

Cook onion, green pepper and red pepper in margarine in skillet over medium heat until tender-crisp. Stir in steak sauce and horseradish; keep warm.

Shape ground beef into 4 burgers. Grill burgers over medium heat for 5 minutes on each side or until desired doneness. Place burgers on roll bottoms; top each with ¼ cup pepper mixture and roll top. Serve immediately. *Makes 4 servings*

Big D Ranch Burger

Hawaiian-Style Burgers

1½ pounds ground beef

⅓ cup chopped green onions

2 tablespoons Worcestershire sauce

⅛ teaspoon black pepper

⅓ cup pineapple preserves

⅓ cup barbecue sauce

6 pineapple slices

6 hamburger buns, split and toasted

1. Combine beef, onions, Worcestershire and pepper in large bowl. Shape into six 1-inch-thick patties.

2. Combine preserves and barbecue sauce in small saucepan. Bring to a boil over medium heat, stirring often.

3. Place patties on grill rack directly above medium coals. Grill, uncovered, until desired doneness, turning and brushing often with sauce. Place pineapple on grill; grill 1 minute or until browned, turning once.

4. To serve, place patties on buns with pineapple.

Makes 6 servings

Broiling Directions: Arrange patties on rack in broiler pan. Broil 4 inches from heat until desired doneness, turning and brushing often with sauce. Broil pineapple 1 minute, turning once.

Magical Tip

Pineapples are the traditional symbol of hospitality, and these burgers are loaded with pineapple flavor. Show your generosity by hosting a luau featuring these tasty burgers.

Hawaiian-Style Burger

Southwest Pesto Burgers

CILANTRO PESTO

  1 large clove garlic

  4 ounces fresh cilantro,
     stems removed and
     rinsed

1½ teaspoons bottled
     minced jalapeño
     pepper *or*
     1 tablespoon bottled
     sliced jalapeño
     pepper,* drained

  ¼ teaspoon salt

  ¼ cup vegetable oil

BURGERS

1¼ pounds ground beef

  ¼ cup plus 1 tablespoon
     Cilantro Pesto, divided

  ½ teaspoon salt

  4 slices pepper jack cheese

  2 tablespoons light or
     regular mayonnaise

  4 Kaiser rolls, split

  1 ripe avocado, peeled and
     sliced

    Salsa

*Jalapeño peppers can sting and irritate the skin; wear rubber gloves when handling peppers and do not touch eyes. Wash hands after handling.

1. For pesto, drop garlic through feed tube of food processor with motor running; process until minced. Add cilantro, jalapeño pepper and ¼ teaspoon salt; process until cilantro is chopped.

2. Slowly add oil through feed tube; process until thick paste forms. Transfer to container with tight-fitting lid. Store in refrigerator up to 3 weeks.

3. To complete recipe, prepare barbecue grill for direct cooking.

4. Combine beef, ¼ cup pesto and ½ teaspoon salt in large bowl; mix well. Form into 4 patties. Place patties on grid over medium-hot coals. Grill, uncovered, 4 to 5 minutes per side or until meat is no longer pink in center. Add cheese to patties during last 1 minute of grilling.

5. While patties are cooking, combine mayonnaise and remaining 1 tablespoon pesto in small bowl; mix well. Top patties with mayonnaise mixture. Serve on rolls with avocado and salsa. *Makes 4 servings*

Serving Suggestion: Serve with refried beans.

Make-Ahead Time: up to 3 weeks in refrigerator
Final Prep and Cook Time: 20 minutes

Southwest Pesto Burger

Meatball Grinders

1 pound ground chicken

½ cup fresh whole wheat or white bread crumbs (1 slice bread)

1 egg white

3 tablespoons finely chopped fresh parsley

2 cloves garlic, minced

¼ teaspoon salt

⅛ teaspoon black pepper

Nonstick cooking spray

¼ cup chopped onion

1 can (8 ounces) whole tomatoes, drained and coarsely chopped

1 can (4 ounces) reduced-sodium tomato sauce

1 teaspoon dried Italian seasoning

4 small hard rolls, split

2 tablespoons grated Parmesan cheese

1. Combine chicken, bread crumbs, egg white, parsley, garlic, salt and pepper in medium bowl. Form mixture into 12 to 16 meatballs. Spray medium nonstick skillet with cooking spray; heat over medium heat until hot. Add meatballs; cook and stir about 5 minutes or until browned on all sides. Remove meatballs from skillet.

2. Add onion to skillet; cook and stir 2 to 3 minutes. Stir in tomatoes, tomato sauce and Italian seasoning; heat to a boil. Reduce heat to low and simmer, covered, 15 minutes. Return meatballs to skillet; simmer, covered, 15 minutes.

3. Place 3 to 4 meatballs in each roll. Divide sauce evenly; spoon over meatballs. Sprinkle with cheese.

Makes 4 servings

Meatball Grinder

Quintessential **Quickies**

Black Gold Burgers

¾ cup finely chopped onion

6 large cloves garlic, minced (about 3 tablespoons)

2 tablespoons margarine

1 tablespoon sugar

¾ cup A.1.® Original® or A.1.® BOLD & SPICY Steak Sauce

1½ pounds ground beef

6 onion rolls, split

In medium skillet, over medium heat, cook and stir onion and garlic in margarine until tender but not brown; stir in sugar. Reduce heat to low; cook for 10 minutes. Stir in steak sauce; keep warm. Shape ground beef into 6 patties. Grill burgers over medium heat for 5 minutes on each side or until done. Place burgers on roll bottoms; top each with 3 tablespoons sauce and roll top. Serve immediately; garnish as desired.   *Makes 6 servings*

Blue Cheese Burgers

1¼ pounds lean ground beef

1 tablespoon finely chopped onion

1½ teaspoons chopped fresh thyme *or* ½ teaspoon dried thyme leaves

¾ teaspoon salt

Dash ground black pepper

4 ounces blue cheese, crumbled

Preheat grill.

Combine ground beef, onion, thyme, salt and pepper in medium bowl; mix lightly. Shape into eight patties.

Place cheese in center of four patties to within ½ inch of outer edge; top with remaining 4 burgers. Press edges together to seal.

Grill 8 minutes or to desired doneness, turning once. Serve with lettuce, tomatoes and Dijon mustard on whole wheat buns, if desired.   *Makes 4 servings*

Black Gold Burger

Grilled Feta Burgers

½ pound lean ground sirloin

½ pound ground turkey breast

2 teaspoons grated lemon peel

1 teaspoon olive oil

1 teaspoon dried oregano leaves

¼ teaspoon salt

⅛ teaspoon black pepper

1 ounce feta cheese

Cucumber Raita (recipe follows)

4 slices tomato

4 whole wheat hamburger buns

1. Combine sirloin, turkey, lemon peel, oil, oregano, salt and pepper; mix well and shape into 8 patties. Make small depression in each of 4 patties and place ¼ of the cheese in each depression. Cover each with remaining 4 patties, sealing edges to form burgers.

2. Grill burgers 10 to 12 minutes or until thoroughly cooked, turning once. Serve with Cucumber Raita and tomato slice on whole wheat bun.   *Makes 4 burgers*

Cucumber Raita

1 cup plain nonfat yogurt

½ cup finely chopped cucumber

1 tablespoon minced fresh mint leaves

1 clove garlic, minced

¼ teaspoon salt

Combine all ingredients in small bowl. Cover and refrigerate until ready to use.

Grilled Feta Burger

Burrito Burgers

6 tablespoons A.1.® Original or A.1.® BOLD & SPICY Steak Sauce, divided

1 (4-ounce) can diced green chilies, divided

3 tablespoons dairy sour cream

1 pound ground beef

4 (6½-inch) flour tortillas

1 medium tomato, sliced

1 cup shredded lettuce

½ cup shredded Cheddar cheese (2 ounces)

Blend 2 tablespoons steak sauce, 2 tablespoons chilies and sour cream. Cover; refrigerate until ready to serve.

Mix beef, remaining ¼ cup steak sauce and chilies. Shape mixture into 4 (4-inch) oval patties. Grill burgers over medium heat or broil 6 inches from heat source 5 minutes on each side or until beef is no longer pink in center. Place each burger in center of 1 tortilla; top evenly with tomato, lettuce, cheese and chilled sauce. Fold edges of tortillas in like a burrito. Serve immediately. *Makes 4 servings*

Burrito Burger

Ranchero Onion Burgers

1 pound ground beef

½ cup salsa

½ cup (2 ounces) shredded Monterey Jack cheese

1 ⅓ cups *French's*® French Fried Onions, divided

½ teaspoon garlic powder

¼ teaspoon ground black pepper

4 hamburger rolls

Combine beef, salsa, cheese, ⅔ *cup* French Fried Onions, garlic powder and pepper in large bowl. Shape into 4 patties.

Place patties on oiled grid. Grill* over medium coals 10 minutes or until no longer pink in center, turning once. Serve on rolls. Garnish with additional salsa, if desired. Top with remaining ⅔ *cup* onions
.

Makes 4 servings

*Or, broil 6 inches from heat.

Tip: For extra-crispy warm onion flavor, heat French Fried Onions in the microwave for 1 minute. Or, place in foil pan and heat on the grill 2 minutes.

Prep Time: 10 minutes
Cook Time: 10 minutes

Ranchero Onion Burger

Mexicali Burgers

Guacamole (recipe
   follows)
1 pound ground beef
⅓ cup prepared salsa or
   picante sauce
⅓ cup crushed tortilla chips
3 tablespoons finely
   chopped fresh cilantro
2 tablespoons finely
   chopped onion
1 teaspoon ground cumin
4 slices Monterey Jack or
   Cheddar cheese
4 Kaiser rolls or hamburger
   buns, split
Lettuce leaves (optional)
Sliced tomatoes
   (optional)

To prevent sticking, spray grill with nonstick cooking spray. Prepare coals for grilling. Meanwhile, prepare Guacamole.

Combine beef, salsa, tortilla chips, cilantro, onion and cumin in medium bowl until well blended. Shape mixture into 4 burgers. Place burgers on grill, 6 inches from medium coals. Grill, covered, 8 to 10 minutes for medium or until desired doneness is reached, turning once. Place 1 slice cheese on each burger during last 1 to 2 minutes of grilling. If desired, place rolls, cut side down, on grill to toast lightly during last 1 to 2 minutes of grilling. Place burgers between rolls; top burgers with Guacamole. Serve with lettuce and tomatoes. Garnish as desired. *Makes 4 servings*

Guacamole

1 ripe avocado, seeded
1 tablespoon salsa or picante sauce
1 teaspoon lime or lemon juice
¼ teaspoon garlic salt

Place avocado in medium bowl; mash with fork until avocado is slightly chunky. Add salsa, lime juice and garlic salt; blend well. *Makes about ½ cup*

Mexicali Burger

Southwestern Sloppy Joes

- 1 pound lean ground round
- 1 cup chopped onion
- ¼ cup chopped celery
- ¼ cup water
- 1 can (10 ounces) diced tomatoes and green chilies, undrained
- 1 can (8 ounces) no-salt-added tomato sauce
- 4 teaspoons brown sugar
- ½ teaspoon ground cumin
- ¼ teaspoon salt
- 9 whole wheat hamburger buns

1. Heat large nonstick skillet over high heat. Add beef, onion, celery and water. Reduce heat to medium. Cook and stir 5 minutes or until meat is no longer pink; drain fat.

2. Stir in tomatoes and green chilies, tomato sauce, brown sugar, cumin and salt; bring to a boil over high heat. Reduce heat; simmer 20 minutes or until mixture thickens. Serve on whole wheat buns. Garnish as desired. *Makes 9 (⅓-cup) servings*

Health Note: Now you can have your beef and heart health, too. Just be sure the beef is lean. Beef is rich in nutrients so it packs a healthy dose of vitamins and minerals. Also, lean beef is a terrific source of iron, zinc and B vitamins.

Southwestern Sloppy Joe

Inside-Out Brie Burgers

1 pound ground beef
5 tablespoons A.1.®
  Original or A.1.® BOLD
  & SPICY Steak Sauce,
  divided
3 ounces Brie, cut into
  4 slices
¼ cup dairy sour cream
2 tablespoons chopped
  green onion
1 medium red bell pepper,
  cut into ¼-inch rings
4 (2½-inch) slices Italian or
  French bread, halved
4 radicchio or lettuce
  leaves

Mix ground beef and 3 tablespoons steak sauce; shape into 8 thin patties. Place 1 slice Brie in center of each of 4 patties. Top with remaining patties. Seal edges to form 4 patties; set aside.

Blend sour cream, remaining 2 tablespoons steak sauce and green onion; set aside.

Grill burgers over medium heat or broil 6 inches from heat source 7 minutes on each side or until beef is no longer pink. Place pepper rings on grill or under broiler; cook with burgers until tender, about 4 to 5 minutes. Top each of 4 bread slice halves with radicchio leaf, pepper ring, burger, 2 tablespoons reserved sauce and another bread slice half. Serve immediately. Garnish as desired. *Makes 4 servings*

Blackened Burgers

1 pound ground beef
5 tablespoons A.1.® Steak
  Sauce, divided
4 teaspoons coarsely
  cracked black pepper,
  divided
4 kaiser rolls, split
4 tomato slices

In medium bowl, combine ground beef, 3 tablespoons steak sauce and 1 teaspoon pepper; shape mixture into 4 patties. Brush patties with remaining 2 tablespoons steak sauce; coat with remaining 3 teaspoons pepper.

Grill burgers over medium heat for 5 minutes on each side or until done. Top each roll bottom with burger, tomato slice and roll top. Serve immediately.

Makes 4 servings

Inside-Out Brie Burger

Beef Burgers with Corn Salsa

½ cup frozen corn

½ cup peeled, seeded and chopped tomato

1 can (4 ounces) diced green chilies, divided

1 tablespoon chopped fresh cilantro *or* 1 teaspoon dried cilantro leaves

1 tablespoon vinegar

1 teaspoon olive oil

¼ cup fine dry bread crumbs

3 tablespoons skim milk

¼ teaspoon garlic powder

12 ounces 95% lean ground beef

Prepare corn according to package directions, omitting salt; drain. Combine corn, tomato, 2 tablespoons green chilies, cilantro, vinegar and oil in small bowl. Cover and refrigerate.

Preheat broiler. Combine bread crumbs, remaining green chilies, skim milk and garlic powder in medium bowl. Add beef; blend well to combine. Shape to form four ¾-inch-thick patties. Place on broiler pan. Broil 4 inches from heat 6 minutes. Turn and broil 6 to 8 minutes more or until beef is no longer pink in center. Spoon salsa over patties. *Makes 4 servings*

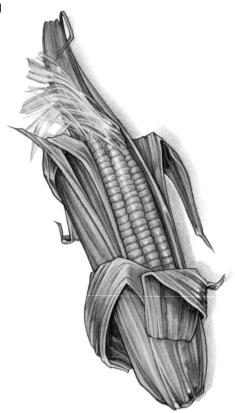

Beef Burgers with Corn Salsa

All-American Stuffed Turkey Burger

1 pound ground turkey

¼ cup uncooked quick rolled oats

1 egg

½ teaspoon garlic powder

Dash ground black pepper

½ cup chopped onion

¼ cup dill pickle relish, drained

2 tablespoons ketchup

2 teaspoons prepared mustard

2 slices (1 ounce each) reduced-calorie low-sodium process American cheese, cut into 4 equal strips

Lettuce leaves (optional)

Tomato slices (optional)

1. Preheat grill for direct-heat grilling.

2. In medium bowl combine turkey, oats, egg, garlic powder and pepper. Divide turkey mixture in half. On 2 (11×10-inch) pieces wax paper, shape each half of turkey mixture into 6-inch-wide patty.

3. Sprinkle onion and relish over one patty, leaving ½-inch border around outside edge; top with ketchup and mustard. Arrange cheese strips, spoke-fashion, over ketchup and mustard. Carefully invert second patty over cheese. Remove top piece wax paper. Press edges together to seal.

4. Lightly grease cold grill rack and position over hot coals. Invert turkey burger onto grill rack; remove wax paper. Grill burger 8 minutes per side or until internal temperature of 165°F is reached on meat thermometer. To turn burger, slide flat cookie sheet under burger and invert onto second flat cookie sheet, then carefully slide burger back onto grill rack.*

5. To serve, cut burger into quarters. Serve with lettuce and tomato, if desired. *Makes 4 servings*

*Can use greased wire grill basket, if desired.

Favorite recipe from **National Turkey Federation**

Beach Blanket Burgers

½ cup MIRACLE WHIP® Salad Dressing

½ teaspoon garlic powder

½ teaspoon onion powder

1 pound ground beef

2 tablespoons dry bread crumbs

¾ teaspoon salt

¼ teaspoon coarse grind black pepper

4 KRAFT® DELI DELUXE® Pasteurized Process American Cheese Slices

4 whole wheat hamburger buns, split, toasted

Lettuce and tomato slices

• **MIX** salad dressing, garlic powder and onion powder; reserve ¼ cup. Mix beef, remaining salad dressing mixture, bread crumbs, salt and pepper. Shape into 4 (½-inch-thick) patties.

• **PLACE** on greased grill over hot coals or on greased rack of broiler pan 5 to 7 inches from heat. Grill or broil 3 to 4 minutes on each side or to desired doneness. Top each patty with 1 process cheese slice; continue grilling or broiling just until process cheese melts.

• **SPREAD** buns with reserved salad dressing mixture; fill with lettuce, tomato slices and patties.

Makes 4 servings

Prep Time: 5 minutes
Grill Time: 10 minutes

Magical Tip

If you've got leftover grilled hamburgers, wrap them tightly in heavy-duty foil and freeze them for up to 4 months. Then unwrap, defrost and heat for that just-grilled taste. Place 1 unwrapped hamburger on a microwavable plate. Heat at MEDIUM (50% power) about 1½ minutes. For 2 hamburgers, heat at MEDIUM (50% power) about 2½ minutes.

Magical Meals

Beefy Bean & Walnut Stir-Fry

1 teaspoon vegetable oil
3 cloves garlic, minced
1 pound lean ground beef
    or ground turkey
1 bag (16 ounces) BIRDS
    EYE® frozen Cut Green
    Beans, thawed
1 teaspoon salt
½ cup walnut pieces

• In large skillet, heat oil and garlic over medium heat about 30 seconds.

• Add beef and beans; sprinkle with salt. Mix well.

• Cook 5 minutes or until beef is well browned, stirring occasionally.

• Stir in walnuts; cook 2 minutes more.

Makes 4 servings

Serving Suggestion: Serve over hot cooked egg noodles or rice.

Birds Eye Idea: When you add California walnuts to Birds Eye® vegetables, you not only add texture and a great nutty taste, but nutrition too.

Prep Time: 5 minutes
Cook Time: 7 to 10 minutes

Beefy Bean & Walnut Stir-Fry

Beefy Nacho Crescent Bake

1 pound lean ground beef

½ cup chopped onion

¼ teaspoon salt

⅛ teaspoon black pepper

1 tablespoon chili powder

1 teaspoon ground cumin

1 teaspoon dried oregano
  leaves

1 can (11 ounces)
  condensed nacho
  cheese soup, undiluted

1 cup milk

1 can (8 ounces)
  refrigerated crescent
  roll dough

¼ cup (1 ounce) shredded
  Cheddar cheese

Chopped fresh cilantro
  (optional)

Salsa (optional)

Preheat oven to 375°F. Spray 13×9-inch baking dish with nonstick cooking spray.

Place beef and onion in large skillet; season with salt and pepper. Brown beef over medium-high heat until no longer pink, stirring to separate meat; drain fat. Stir in chili powder, cumin and oregano. Cook and stir 2 minutes; remove from heat.

Combine soup and milk in medium bowl, stirring until smooth. Pour soup mixture into prepared dish, spreading evenly.

Separate crescent dough into 4 rectangles; firmly press perforations together. Roll each rectangle to 8×4 inches. Cut each rectangle in half crosswise to form 8 (4-inch) squares.

Spoon about ¼ cup beef mixture in center of each square. Lift 4 corners of dough up over filling to meet in center; pinch and twist firmly to seal. Place squares in dish.

Bake, uncovered, 20 to 25 minutes or until crusts are golden brown. Sprinkle cheese over squares. Bake 5 minutes or until cheese melts. To serve, spoon soup mixture in dish over each serving; sprinkle with cilantro and serve with salsa, if desired. *Makes 4 servings*

Beefy Nacho Crescent Bake

Italian-Style Meat Loaf

1 egg
1½ pounds lean ground beef
   or turkey
8 ounces hot or mild Italian
   sausage, casings
   removed
1 cup CONTADINA®
   Seasoned Bread
   Crumbs
1 can (8 ounces)
   CONTADINA Tomato
   Sauce, divided
1 cup finely chopped onion
½ cup finely chopped green
   bell pepper

1. Beat egg lightly in large bowl. Add beef, sausage, bread crumbs, ¾ cup tomato sauce, onion and bell pepper; mix well.

2. Press into ungreased 9×5-inch loaf pan. Bake, uncovered, in preheated 350°F oven for 60 minutes.

3. Spoon remaining tomato sauce over meat loaf. Bake 15 minutes longer or until no longer pink in center; drain. Let stand for 10 minutes before serving.

Makes 8 servings

Prep Time: 10 minutes
Cook Time: 75 minutes
Standing Time: 10 minutes

Stuffed French Bread

1 pound ground beef
1 package (1¼ ounces)
   taco seasoning mix
1 loaf French bread, cut in
   half lengthwise
⅔ cup chopped lettuce
⅔ cup chopped pitted ripe
   olives
⅔ cup chopped green bell
   pepper
⅔ cup chopped tomato
⅔ cup tortilla chips,
   crushed
⅔ cup taco flavored cheese
   Taco sauce (optional)
   Sour cream (optional)

Brown ground beef and drain. Add taco seasoning. Hollow out French bread halves to form shell. Layer ground beef mixture, lettuce, black olives, bell pepper and tomato in bottom half of loaf. Top with tortilla chips, cheese and top half of loaf. Heat stuffed loaf in microwave oven just until cheese melts. Cut into quarters and serve with taco sauce and sour cream, if desired.

Makes 4 servings

Favorite recipe from **North Dakota Beef Commission**

Italian-Style Meat Loaf

30-Minute Chili Olé

1 cup chopped onion

2 cloves garlic, minced

1 tablespoon vegetable oil

2 pounds ground beef

1 (15-ounce) can tomato sauce

1 (14½-ounce) can stewed tomatoes

¾ cup A.1.® Steak Sauce

1 tablespoon chili powder

1 teaspoon ground cumin

1 (16-ounce) can black beans, rinsed and drained

1 (11-ounce) can corn, drained

Shredded cheese, sour cream and chopped tomato, for garnish

Sauté onion and garlic in oil in 6-quart heavy pot over medium-high heat until tender.

Add beef; cook and stir until brown. Drain; stir in tomato sauce, stewed tomatoes, steak sauce, chili powder and cumin.

Heat to a boil; reduce heat to low. Cover; simmer for 10 minutes, stirring occasionally. Stir in beans and corn; simmer, uncovered, for 10 minutes.

Serve hot, garnished with cheese, sour cream and tomatoes.

Makes 8 servings

30-Minute Chili Olé

Joe's Special

1 pound lean ground beef

2 cups sliced mushrooms

1 small onion, chopped

2 teaspoons Worcestershire sauce

1 teaspoon dried oregano leaves

1 teaspoon ground nutmeg

½ teaspoon garlic powder

½ teaspoon salt

1 package (10 ounces) frozen chopped spinach, thawed

4 large eggs, lightly beaten

⅓ cup grated Parmesan cheese

1. Spray large skillet with nonstick cooking spray. Add ground beef, mushrooms and onion; cook over medium-high heat 6 to 8 minutes or until onion is tender, breaking beef apart with wooden spoon. Add Worcestershire, oregano, nutmeg, garlic powder and salt. Cook until meat is no longer pink.

2. Drain spinach (do not squeeze dry); stir into meat mixture. Push mixture to one side of pan. Reduce heat to medium. Pour eggs into other side of pan; cook, without stirring, 1 to 2 minutes or until set on bottom. Lift eggs to allow uncooked portion to flow underneath. Repeat until softly set. Gently stir into meat mixture and heat through. Stir in cheese.

Makes 4 to 6 servings

Serving Suggestion: Serve with salsa and toast.

Prep and Cook Time: 20 minutes

Joe's Special

Hearty Ground Beef Stew

1 pound ground beef
3 cloves garlic, minced
1 package (16 ounces)
  Italian-style frozen
  vegetables
2 cups southern-style hash
  brown potatoes
1 jar (14 ounces) marinara
  sauce
1 can (10½ ounces)
  condensed beef broth
3 tablespoons *French's*®
  Worcestershire Sauce

1. Brown beef with garlic in large saucepan; drain. Add remaining ingredients. Heat to boiling. Cover. Reduce heat to medium-low. Cook 10 minutes or until vegetables are crisp-tender.

2. Serve in warm bowls with garlic bread, if desired.

Makes 6 servings

Prep Time: 5 minutes
Cook Time: 15 minutes

15 Minute Cheeseburger Rice

1 pound ground beef
1¾ cups water
⅔ cup catsup
1 tablespoon KRAFT® Pure
  Prepared Mustard
2 cups MINUTE® White Rice,
  uncooked
1 cup KRAFT® Shredded
  Cheddar Cheese

BROWN meat in large skillet; drain.

ADD water, catsup and mustard. Bring to boil.

STIR in rice. Sprinkle with cheese; cover. Cook on low heat 5 minutes.

Makes 4 servings

Prep Time: 5 minutes
Cook Time: 15 minutes

Hearty Ground Beef Stew

Spaghetti Rolls

1 package (8 ounces)
   manicotti shells
2 pounds ground beef
1 tablespoon onion powder
1 teaspoon salt
½ teaspoon black pepper
2 cups spaghetti sauce,
   divided
1 cup (4 ounces) shredded
   pizza-flavored cheese
   blend or mozzarella
   cheese

1. Cook pasta according to package directions. Place in colander; rinse under warm running water. Drain well.

2. Preheat oven to 350°F. Grease 13×9-inch baking pan.

3. Cook beef in large skillet over medium-high heat until brown, stirring to separate meat; drain drippings. Stir in onion powder, salt and pepper. Stir in 1 cup spaghetti sauce; cool and set aside.

4. Reserve ½ cup ground beef mixture. Combine remaining beef mixture with cheese in large bowl. Fill shells with remaining beef mixture using spoon.

5. Arrange shells in prepared pan. Combine remaining 1 cup spaghetti sauce with reserved beef mixture in small bowl; blend well. Pour over shells. Cover with foil.

6. Bake 20 to 30 minutes or until hot. Garnish as desired.

Makes 4 servings

Magical Tip

If the pasta sticks together after cooking, here's a little kitchen wizardry to make the problem magically disappear: toss the pasta very briefly with hot running water. Drain it thoroughly, as excess cooking water will dilute the sauce.

Spaghetti Rolls

Quick Chunky Chili

Magical **Meals**

1 pound lean ground beef

1 medium onion, chopped

1 tablespoon chili powder

1½ teaspoons ground cumin

2 cans (16 ounces each) diced tomatoes, undrained

1 can (15 ounces) pinto beans, drained

½ cup prepared salsa

½ cup (2 ounces) shredded Cheddar cheese

3 tablespoons sour cream

4 teaspoons sliced black olives

Combine meat and onion in 3-quart saucepan; cook over high heat until meat is no longer pink, breaking meat apart with wooden spoon. Add chili powder and cumin; stir 1 minute or until fragrant. Add tomatoes, beans and salsa. Bring to a boil; stir constantly. Reduce heat to low; simmer, covered, 10 minutes. Ladle into bowls. Top with cheese, sour cream and olives.

Makes 4 (1½-cup) servings

Serving Suggestion: Serve with tossed green salad and cornbread muffins.

Prep and Cook Time: 25 minutes

Mama's Best Ever Spaghetti & Meatballs

1 pound lean ground beef

½ cup Italian seasoned dry bread crumbs

1 egg

1 jar (26 to 28 ounces) RAGÚ® Old World Style® Pasta Sauce

8 ounces spaghetti, cooked and drained

1. In medium bowl, combine ground beef, bread crumbs and egg; shape into 12 meatballs.

2. In 3-quart saucepan, bring Ragú Pasta Sauce to a boil over medium-high heat. Gently stir in meatballs.

3. Reduce heat to low and simmer covered, stirring occasionally, 20 minutes or until meatballs are done. Serve over hot spaghetti. *Makes 4 servings*

Prep Time: 10 minutes
Cook Time: 20 minutes

Quick Chunky Chili

Meatball Stroganoff with Rice

MEATBALLS
    1 egg, lightly beaten
    1½ pounds ground beef
    ⅓ cup plain dry bread
        crumbs
    1 tablespoon
        Worcestershire sauce
    1 teaspoon salt
    ¼ teaspoon pepper
    2 tablespoons CRISCO® Oil*

SAUCE
    1 tablespoon CRISCO® Oil
    ½ pound mushrooms, sliced
    2 tablespoons all-purpose
        flour
    1 teaspoon ketchup
    1 can (10½ ounces)
        condensed, double
        strength beef broth
        (bouillon), undiluted**
    ½ (1-ounce) envelope dry
        onion soup mix (about
        2 tablespoons)
    1 cup sour cream
    4 cups hot cooked rice

*Use your favorite Crisco Oil product.

**1¼ cups reconstituted beef broth
made with double amount of very low
sodium beef broth granules may be
substituted for beef broth (bouillon).

1. For meatballs, combine egg, meat, bread crumbs, Worcestershire sauce, salt and pepper in large bowl. Mix until well blended. Shape into eighteen 2-inch meatballs.

2. Heat 2 tablespoons oil in large skillet on medium heat. Add meatballs. Brown on all sides. Reduce heat to low. Cook 10 minutes. Remove meatballs from skillet.

3. For sauce, add 1 tablespoon oil to skillet. Add mushrooms. Cook and stir 4 minutes. Remove skillet from heat.

4. Stir in flour and ketchup until blended. Stir in broth gradually. Add soup mix. Return to heat. Bring to a boil on medium heat. Reduce heat to low. Simmer 2 minutes. Return meatballs to skillet. Heat thoroughly, stirring occasionally.

5. Stir in sour cream. Heat but do not bring to a boil. Serve over hot rice. Garnish, if desired.

Makes 6 servings

Meatball Stroganoff with Rice

Souperior Meat Loaf

2 pounds ground beef

¾ cup plain dry bread
  crumbs*

1 envelope LIPTON® RECIPE
  SECRETS® Onion Soup
  Mix**

¾ cup water

⅓ cup ketchup

2 eggs

*Substitution: Use 1 ½ cups fresh bread crumbs or 5 slices fresh bread, cubed.

**Also terrific with LIPTON® RECIPE SECRETS® Beefy Onion, Onion Mushroom, Beefy Mushroom or Savory Herb with Garlic Soup Mix.

1. Preheat oven to 350°F. In large bowl, combine all ingredients.

2. In 13×9-inch baking or roasting pan, shape into loaf.

3. Bake uncovered 1 hour or until done. Let stand 10 minutes before serving. *Makes 8 servings*

Slow Cooker Method: Place meat loaf in slow cooker. Cover. Cook on HIGH for 4 hours or LOW 6 to 8 hours.

Helpful Hint: Placing meat loaf on a piece of cheesecloth and then on a rack helps to hold the meat together while lifting in and out of slow cooker.

Recipe Tip: It's a snap to make fresh bread crumbs. Simply place fresh or day old white, Italian or French bread in a food processor or blender, and process until fine crumbs form.

Prep Time: 10 minutes
Cook Time: 1 hour

Magical **Meals**

Souperior Meat Loaf

Beef with Snow Peas & Baby Corn

¾ pound extra-lean (90% lean) ground beef

1 clove garlic, minced

1 teaspoon vegetable oil

6 ounces snow peas, halved lengthwise

1 red bell pepper, cut into strips

1 can (15 ounces) baby corn, drained, rinsed

1 tablespoon soy sauce

1 teaspoon sesame oil

Salt and black pepper

2 cups cooked rice

Brown ground beef in wok or large skillet; drain. Add garlic; cook until tender. Set aside. Wipe out wok with paper towel.

Heat vegetable oil in wok over medium-high heat. Add snow peas and red bell pepper; stir-fry 2 to 3 minutes or until vegetables are crisp-tender. Stir in ground beef mixture, baby corn, soy sauce and sesame oil. Season with salt and black pepper to taste. Serve over rice.

Makes 4 servings

Magical Tip

Baby corn has long been a popular ingredient in Asian and Asian-style cooking, but is newer to American cuisine. This vegetable's miniature size involves no hocus-pocus of genetic engineering. Baby corn is just that—the immature, tender cobs of sweet corn, harvested when the ear begins to develop.

Beef with Snow Peas & Baby Corn

Italian Meat Loaf Patties

2 packages (12 ounces each) extra-wide noodles

2 tablespoons butter or margarine, melted

1 can (15 ounces) DEL MONTE® Original Sloppy Joe Sauce

2 pounds ground beef or turkey

1 cup dry Italian seasoned bread crumbs

2 eggs, beaten

1 tablespoon dried minced onion

1. Preheat oven to 375°F.

2. Cook noodles according to package directions; drain. Toss with butter; keep hot.

3. Set aside half of sauce to brush on patties. In large bowl, combine remaining sauce with remaining ingredients; mix with fork. On large, greased baking sheet, shape meat mixture into 8 (1-inch-thick) oblong patties. Brush reserved sauce over patties.

4. Bake 20 minutes or until no longer pink in center. Serve patties with hot, buttered noodles. Garnish, if desired. *Makes 8 servings*

Prep Time: 5 minutes
Cook Time: 20 minutes

Italian Meat Loaf Patties

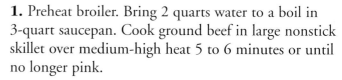

Chili-Stuffed Poblano Peppers

Magical **Meals**

1 pound lean ground beef

4 large poblano peppers

1 can (15 ounces) chili-seasoned beans

1 can (14½ ounces) chili-style chunky tomatoes, undrained

1 tablespoon Mexican (Adobo) seasoning

⅔ cup shredded Mexican cheese blend or Monterey Jack cheese

1. Preheat broiler. Bring 2 quarts water to a boil in 3-quart saucepan. Cook ground beef in large nonstick skillet over medium-high heat 5 to 6 minutes or until no longer pink.

2. While meat is cooking, cut peppers in half lengthwise; remove stems and seeds. Add 4 pepper halves to boiling water; cook 3 minutes or until bright green and slightly softened. Remove; drain upside down on plate. Repeat with remaining 4 halves. Set aside.

3. Add beans, tomatoes and Mexican seasoning to ground beef. Cook and stir over medium heat 5 minutes or until mixture slightly thickens.

4. Arrange peppers, cut sides up, in 13×9-inch baking dish. Divide chili mixture evenly among each pepper; top with cheese. Broil 6 inches from heat 1 minute or until cheese is melted. Serve immediately.

Makes 4 servings

Serving Suggestion: Serve with cornbread and chunky salsa.

Prep and Cook Time: 26 minutes

Chili-Stuffed Poblano Peppers

Blue Cheese Burgers with Red Onion

Magical **Meals**

2 pounds ground chuck

2 cloves garlic, minced

1 teaspoon salt

½ teaspoon black pepper

4 ounces blue cheese

⅓ cup coarsely chopped
　　walnuts, toasted

1 torpedo (long) red onion
　　or 2 small red onions,
　　sliced into ⅜-inch-thick
　　rounds

2 baguettes (each
　　12 inches long)

　　Olive or vegetable oil

Combine beef, garlic, salt and pepper in medium bowl. Shape meat mixture into 12 oval patties. Mash cheese and blend with walnuts in small bowl. Divide cheese mixture equally; place onto centers of 6 meat patties. Top with remaining meat patties; tightly pinch edges together to seal in filling.

Oil hot grid to help prevent sticking. Grill patties and onion, if desired, on covered grill, over medium KINGSFORD® Briquets, 7 to 12 minutes for medium doneness, turning once. Cut baguettes into 4-inch lengths; split each piece and brush cut side with olive oil. Move cooked burgers to edge of grill to keep warm. Grill bread, oil side down, until lightly toasted. Serve burgers on toasted baguettes. *Makes 6 servings*

Pasta Pronto

8 ounces linguine or
　　spaghetti, uncooked

1 pound ground beef,
　　ground turkey or mild
　　Italian sausage

1 cup coarsely chopped
　　onions

1 clove garlic, minced

2 cans (14½ ounces each)
　　DEL MONTE® Diced
　　Tomatoes with Basil,
　　Garlic & Oregano

1 can (8 ounces) DEL
　　MONTE Tomato Sauce

　　About ¼ cup (1 ounce)
　　grated Parmesan
　　cheese

1. Cook pasta according to package directions; drain and keep hot.

2. In large skillet, brown meat with onions and garlic; drain.

3. Add undrained tomatoes and tomato sauce. Cook, stirring frequently, 15 minutes.

4. Spoon sauce over hot pasta; sprinkle with cheese. Serve with French bread, if desired.

Makes 4 servings

Prep Time: 10 minutes
Cook Time: 20 minutes

Blue Cheese Burger with Red Onion

Tacos in Pasta Shells

1 package (3 ounces)
   cream cheese with
   chives

18 jumbo pasta shells

1¼ pounds ground beef

1 teaspoon salt

1 teaspoon chili powder

2 tablespoons butter,
   melted

1 cup prepared taco sauce

1 cup (4 ounces) shredded
   Cheddar cheese

1 cup (4 ounces) shredded
   Monterey Jack cheese

1½ cups crushed tortilla
   chips

1 cup sour cream

3 green onions, chopped

Leaf lettuce, small pitted
   ripe olives and cherry
   tomatoes for garnish

1. Cut cream cheese into ½-inch cubes. Let stand at room temperature until softened. Cook pasta according to package directions. Place in colander and rinse under warm running water; drain well. Return to saucepan.

2. Preheat oven to 350°F. Butter 13×9-inch baking pan.

3. Cook beef in large skillet over medium-high heat until brown, stirring to separate meat; drain drippings. Reduce heat to medium-low. Add cream cheese, salt and chili powder; simmer 5 minutes.

4. Toss shells with butter. Fill shells with beef mixture using spoon. Arrange shells in prepared pan. Pour taco sauce over each shell. Cover with foil.

5. Bake 15 minutes. Uncover; top with Cheddar cheese, Monterey Jack cheese and chips. Bake 15 minutes more or until bubbly. Top with sour cream and onions. Garnish, if desired. *Makes 4 to 6 servings*

Tacos in Pasta Shells

Captivating Casseroles

Heartland Shepherd's Pie

¾ **pound ground beef**

1 **medium onion, chopped**

1 **can (14½ ounces) DEL MONTE® Original Recipe Stewed Tomatoes**

1 **can (8 ounces) DEL MONTE Tomato Sauce**

1 **can (14½ ounces) DEL MONTE Mixed Vegetables, drained**

Instant mashed potato flakes plus ingredients to prepare (enough for 6 servings)

3 **cloves garlic, minced (optional)**

1. Preheat oven to 375°F. In large skillet, brown meat and onion over medium-high heat; drain.

2. Add tomatoes and tomato sauce; cook over high heat until thickened, stirring frequently. Stir in mixed vegetables. Season with salt and pepper, if desired.

3. Spoon into 2-quart baking dish; set aside. Prepare 6 servings mashed potatoes according to package directions, first cooking garlic in specified amount of butter.

4. Top meat mixture with potatoes. Bake 20 minutes or until heated through. Garnish with chopped parsley, if desired. *Makes 4 to 6 servings*

Prep Time: 5 minutes
Cook Time: 30 minutes

Heartland Shepherd's Pie

Old-Fashioned Beef Pot Pie

1 pound ground beef

1 can (11 ounces) condensed beef with vegetables and barley soup, undiluted

½ cup water

1 package (10 ounces) frozen peas and carrots, thawed and drained

½ teaspoon seasoned salt

⅛ teaspoon garlic powder

⅛ teaspoon ground black pepper

1 cup (4 ounces) shredded Cheddar cheese, divided

1⅓ cups *French's*® French Fried Onions, divided

1 package (7.5 ounces) refrigerated biscuits

Preheat oven to 350°F. In large skillet, brown ground beef in large chunks; drain. Stir in soup, water, vegetables and seasonings; bring to a boil. Reduce heat and simmer, uncovered, 5 minutes. Remove from heat; stir in ½ cup cheese and ⅔ *cup* French Fried Onions.

Pour mixture into 12×8-inch baking dish. Cut each biscuit in half; place, cut side down, around edge of casserole. Bake, uncovered, 15 to 20 minutes or until biscuits are done. Top with remaining ½ cup cheese and ⅔ cup onions; bake, uncovered, 5 minutes or until onions are golden brown. *Makes 4 to 6 servings*

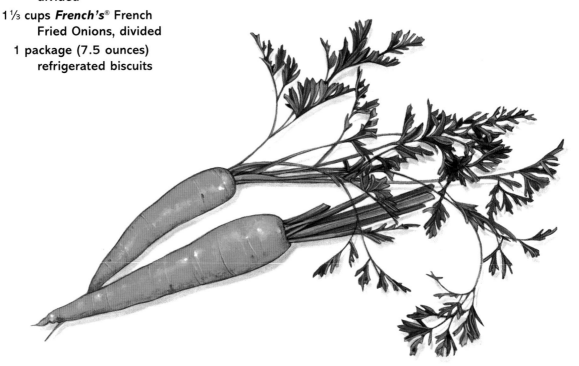

Old-Fashioned Beef Pot Pie

Lasagna Beef 'n' Spinach Roll-Ups

1½ **pounds ground beef**

1 **(28-ounce) jar spaghetti sauce**

½ **cup A.1.® Original or A.1.® BOLD & SPICY Steak Sauce**

½ **teaspoon dried basil leaves**

1 **(15-ounce) container ricotta cheese**

1 **(10-ounce) package frozen chopped spinach, thawed, well drained**

2 **cups shredded mozzarella cheese (8 ounces)**

⅓ **cup grated Parmesan cheese, divided**

1 **egg, beaten**

12 **lasagna noodles, cooked, drained**

2 **tablespoons chopped fresh parsley**

Brown beef in large skillet over medium-high heat until no longer pink, stirring occasionally to break up beef; drain. Mix spaghetti sauce, steak sauce and basil in small bowl; stir 1 cup spaghetti sauce mixture into beef. Set aside remaining sauce mixture.

Mix ricotta cheese, spinach, mozzarella cheese, 3 tablespoons Parmesan cheese and egg in medium bowl. On each lasagna noodle, spread about ¼ cup ricotta mixture. Top with about ⅓ cup beef mixture. Roll up each noodle from short end; lay each roll, seam side down, in lightly greased 13×9×2-inch baking dish. Pour reserved spaghetti sauce mixture over noodles. Sprinkle with remaining Parmesan cheese and parsley.

Bake, covered, at 350°F 30 minutes. Uncover and bake 15 to 20 minutes more or until hot and bubbly. Serve with additional Parmesan cheese, if desired. Garnish as desired.

Makes 6 servings

Lasagna Beef 'n' Spinach Roll-Ups

Pizza Pie Meatloaf

2 pounds ground beef

1½ cups shredded
    mozzarella cheese,
    divided

½ cup unseasoned dry
    bread crumbs

1 cup tomato sauce,
    divided

¼ cup grated Parmesan
    cheese

¼ cup *French's*®
    Worcestershire Sauce

1 tablespoon dried
    oregano leaves

1⅓ cups *French's*® French
    Fried Onions

1. Preheat oven to 350°F. Combine beef, ½ *cup* mozzarella, bread crumbs, ½ *cup* tomato sauce, Parmesan cheese, Worcestershire and oregano in large bowl; stir with fork until well blended.

2. Place meat mixture into round pizza pan with edge or pie plate and shape into 9×1-inch round. Bake 35 minutes or until no longer pink in center and internal temperature reads 160°F. Drain fat.

3. Top with remaining tomato sauce, mozzarella cheese and French Fried Onions. Bake 5 minutes or until cheese is melted and onions are golden. Cut into wedges to serve. *Makes 6 to 8 servings*

Prep Time: 10 minutes
Cook Time: 40 minutes

Pizza Meat Loaf

Zesty Italian Stuffed Peppers

3 bell peppers (green, red or yellow)

1 pound ground beef

1 jar (14 ounces) spaghetti sauce

1⅓ cups *French's*® French Fried Onions, divided

2 tablespoons *Frank's*® *RedHot*® Cayenne Pepper Sauce

½ cup uncooked instant rice

¼ cup sliced ripe olives

1 cup (4 ounces) shredded mozzarella cheese

Preheat oven to 400°F. Cut bell peppers in half lengthwise through stems; discard seeds. Place pepper halves, cut sides up, in 2-quart shallow baking dish; set aside.

Place beef in large microwavable bowl. Microwave on HIGH 5 minutes or until meat is browned, stirring once; drain. Stir in spaghetti sauce, ⅔ *cup* French Fried Onions, *Frank's RedHot* Sauce, rice and olives. Spoon evenly into bell pepper halves.

Cover; bake 35 minutes or until bell peppers are tender. Uncover; sprinkle with cheese and remaining ⅔ *cup* onions. Bake 1 minute or until onions are golden.

Makes 6 servings

Prep Time: 10 minutes
Cook Time: 36 minutes

Zesty Italian Stuffed Pepper

Quick Tamale Casserole

1½ pounds ground beef

¾ cup sliced green onions

1 can (4 ounces) chopped green chilies, drained and divided

1 can (16 ounces) whole kernel corn, drained

1 can (10¾ ounces) condensed tomato soup

¾ cup salsa

1 can (2¼ ounces) chopped pitted ripe olives (optional)

1 tablespoon Worcestershire sauce

1 teaspoon chili powder

¼ teaspoon garlic powder

4 slices (¾ ounce each) American cheese, halved

4 corn muffins, cut into ½-inch cubes

Mexican Sour Cream Topping (recipe follows, optional)

In medium skillet, brown ground beef with green onions. Reserve 2 tablespoons chilies for Mexican Sour Cream Topping, if desired. Stir in remaining chilies, corn, tomato soup, salsa, olives, Worcestershire, chili powder and garlic powder until well blended. Place in 2-quart casserole. Top with cheese, then evenly spread muffin cubes over cheese. Bake at 350°F for 5 to 10 minutes or until cheese is melted. Serve with Mexican Sour Cream Topping, if desired.

Makes 6 servings

Mexican Sour Cream Topping

1 cup sour cream

2 tablespoons chopped green chilies, reserved from above

2 teaspoons chopped jalapeño peppers* (optional)

2 teaspoons lime juice

*Jalapeño peppers can sting and irritate the skin; wear rubber gloves when handling peppers and do not touch eyes. Wash hands after handling.

Combine all ingredients in small bowl; mix until well blended.

Makes about 1 cup

Quick Tamale Casserole

Contadina® Classic Lasagne

Captivating **Casseroles**

1 pound dry lasagne
   noodles, cooked

1 tablespoon olive or
   vegetable oil

1 cup chopped onion

½ cup chopped green bell
   pepper

2 cloves garlic, minced

1½ pounds lean ground beef

2 cans (14.5 ounces each)
   CONTADINA® Recipe
   Ready Diced Tomatoes,
   undrained

1 can (8 ounces)
   CONTADINA Tomato
   Sauce

1 can (6 ounces)
   CONTADINA Tomato
   Paste

½ cup dry red wine or beef
   broth

1½ teaspoons salt

1 teaspoon dried oregano
   leaves, crushed

1 teaspoon dried basil
   leaves, crushed

½ teaspoon ground black
   pepper

1 egg

1 cup (8 ounces) ricotta
   cheese

2 cups (8 ounces)
   shredded mozzarella
   cheese, divided

1. Cook pasta according to package directions; drain.

2. Meanwhile, heat oil in large skillet. Add onion, bell pepper and garlic; sauté for 3 minutes or until vegetables are tender.

3. Add beef; cook for 5 to 6 minutes or until evenly browned.

4. Add tomatoes with juice, tomato sauce, tomato paste, wine, salt, oregano, basil and black pepper; bring to a boil. Reduce heat to low; simmer, uncovered, for 20 minutes, stirring occasionally.

5. Beat egg slightly in medium bowl. Stir in ricotta cheese and 1 cup mozzarella cheese.

6. Layer noodles, half of meat sauce, noodles, all of ricotta cheese mixture, noodles and remaining meat sauce in ungreased 13×9-inch baking dish. Sprinkle with remaining 1 cup mozzarella cheese.

7. Bake in preheated 350°F oven for 25 to 30 minutes or until heated through. Let stand for 10 minutes before cutting to serve. *Makes 10 servings*

Prep Time: 35 minutes
Cook Time: 30 minutes
Standing Time: 10 minutes

Contadina® Classic Lasagne

Beef Stroganoff Casserole

1 pound lean ground beef
¼ teaspoon salt
⅛ teaspoon black pepper
1 teaspoon vegetable oil
8 ounces sliced mushrooms
1 large onion, chopped
3 cloves garlic, minced
¼ cup dry white wine
1 can (10¾ ounces) condensed cream of mushroom soup, undiluted
½ cup sour cream
1 tablespoon Dijon mustard
4 cups cooked egg noodles
Chopped fresh parsley (optional)

Preheat oven to 350°F. Spray 13×9-inch baking dish with nonstick cooking spray.

Place beef in large skillet; season with salt and pepper. Brown beef over medium-high heat until no longer pink, stirring to separate beef. Drain fat from skillet; set beef aside.

Heat oil in same skillet over medium-high heat until hot. Add mushrooms, onion and garlic; cook and stir 2 minutes or until onion is tender. Add wine. Reduce heat to medium-low and simmer 3 minutes. Remove from heat; stir in soup, sour cream and mustard until well combined. Return beef to skillet.

Place noodles in prepared dish. Pour beef mixture over noodles; stir until noodles are well coated.

Bake, uncovered, 30 minutes or until heated through. Sprinkle with parsley, if desired. *Makes 6 servings*

Beef Stroganoff Casserole

Layered Mexican Casserole

8 ounces ground beef

1 (12-ounce) can whole
    kernel corn, drained

1 (12-ounce) jar chunky
    salsa

1 (2¼-ounce) can sliced
    pitted ripe olives,
    drained

1 cup cream-style cottage
    cheese

1 (8-ounce) carton sour
    cream

5 cups tortilla chips (7 to
    8 ounces)

2 cups (8 ounces)
    shredded Wisconsin
    Cheddar cheese,
    divided

½ cup chopped tomato

Brown ground beef in large skillet; drain. Add corn and salsa; cook until thoroughly heated. Reserve 2 tablespoons olives; stir remaining olives into beef mixture. Combine cottage cheese and sour cream in bowl.

In 2-quart casserole, layer 2 cups chips, half of meat mixture, ¾ cup Cheddar cheese and half of cottage cheese mixture. Repeat layers; cover. Bake in preheated 350°F oven, 35 minutes. Line edge of casserole with remaining 1 cup chips; top with tomato, reserved 2 tablespoons olives and remaining ½ cup Cheddar cheese. Bake 10 minutes or until cheese is melted and chips are hot. *Makes 4 to 6 servings*

Favorite recipe from **Wisconsin Milk Marketing Board**

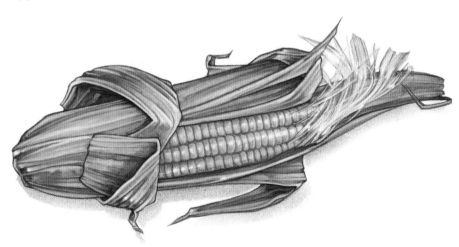

Layered Mexican Casserole

Campbell's® Garlic Mashed Potatoes & Beef Bake

1 pound ground beef
1 can (10¾ ounces)
    CAMPBELL'S®
    Condensed Cream of
    Mushroom with
    Roasted Garlic Soup
1 tablespoon
    Worcestershire sauce
1 bag (16 ounces) frozen
    vegetable combination
    (broccoli, cauliflower,
    carrots), thawed
3 cups hot mashed
    potatoes

1. In medium skillet over medium-high heat, cook beef until browned, stirring to separate meat. Pour off fat.

2. In 2-quart shallow baking dish mix beef, ½ *can* soup, Worcestershire and vegetables.

3. Stir remaining soup into potatoes. Spoon potato mixture over beef mixture. Bake at 400°F. for 20 minutes or until hot.   *Makes 4 servings*

Prep Time: 10 minutes
Cook Time: 20 minutes

Chili Cornbread Casserole

1 pound ground beef
1 medium onion, chopped
1 jar (16 ounces) RAGÚ®
    Cheese Creations!®
    Double Cheddar Sauce
1 can (19 ounces) red
    kidney beans, rinsed
    and drained
1 can (8¾ ounces) whole
    kernel corn, drained
2 to 3 teaspoons chili
    powder
1 package (12 ounces)
    cornbread mix

1. Preheat oven to 400°F. In 12-inch skillet, brown ground beef and onion over medium-high heat; drain. Stir in Ragú Cheese Creations! Sauce, beans, corn and chili powder.

2. Meanwhile, prepare cornbread mix according to package directions. Do not bake.

3. In ungreased 2-quart baking dish, spread ground beef mixture. Top with cornbread mixture. Bake uncovered 20 minutes or until toothpick inserted in center of cornbread comes out clean and top is golden.
                Makes 6 servings

Prep Time: 10 minutes
Cook Time: 20 minutes

Campbell's® Garlic Mashed Potatoes & Beef Bake

Main-Dish Pie

1 package (8 rolls)
   refrigerated crescent
   rolls

1 pound lean ground beef

1 medium onion, chopped

1 can (12 ounces) beef or
   mushroom gravy

1 box (10 ounces) BIRDS
   EYE® frozen Green
   Peas, thawed

½ cup shredded Swiss
   cheese

6 slices tomato

• Preheat oven to 350°F.

• Unroll dough and separate rolls. Spread to cover bottom of ungreased 9-inch pie pan. Press together to form lower crust. Bake 10 minutes.

• Meanwhile, in large skillet, brown beef and onion; drain excess fat.

• Stir in gravy and peas; cook until heated through.

• Pour mixture into partially baked crust. Sprinkle with cheese.

• Bake 10 to 15 minutes or until crust is brown and cheese is melted.

• Arrange tomato slices over pie; bake 2 minutes more.

Makes 6 servings

Prep Time: 10 minutes
Cook Time: 20 to 25 minutes

Main-Dish Pie

California Tamale Pie

1 pound ground beef

1 cup yellow cornmeal

2 cups milk

2 eggs, beaten

1 package (1.48 ounces) LAWRY'S® Spices & Seasonings for Chili

2 teaspoons LAWRY'S® Seasoned Salt

1 can (17 ounces) whole kernel corn, drained

1 can (14½ ounces) whole tomatoes, cut up

1 can (2¼ ounces) sliced ripe olives, drained

1 cup (4 ounces) shredded cheddar cheese

In medium skillet, cook ground beef until browned and crumbly; drain fat. In 2½-quart casserole dish, combine cornmeal, milk and eggs; mix well. Add ground beef and remaining ingredients except cheese; stir to mix. Bake, uncovered, in 350°F oven 1 hour and 15 minutes. Add cheese and continue baking until cheese melts. Let stand 10 minutes before serving.

MICROWAVE OVEN METHOD

In 2½-quart glass casserole, microwave ground beef on HIGH 5 to 6 minutes; drain fat and crumble beef. Mix in cornmeal, milk and eggs; blend well. Add remaining ingredients except cheese. Cover with plastic wrap, venting one corner. Microwave on HIGH 15 minutes, stirring after 8 minutes. Sprinkle cheese over top and microwave on HIGH 2 minutes. Let stand 10 minutes before serving. *Makes 6 to 8 servings*

Serving Suggestion: Serve with mixed green salad flavored with kiwi and green onion.

Hint: Substitute 1 package (1.25 ounces) LAWRY'S® Taco Spices & Seasonings for Spices & Seasonings for Chili, if desired.

California Tamale Pie

Patchwork Casserole

2 pounds ground beef

2 cups chopped green bell peppers

1 cup chopped onion

2 pounds frozen Southern-style hash-brown potatoes, thawed

2 cans (8 ounces each) tomato sauce

1 cup water

1 can (6 ounces) tomato paste

1 teaspoon salt

½ teaspoon dried basil, crumbled

¼ teaspoon black pepper

1 pound pasteurized process American cheese, thinly sliced, divided

Preheat oven to 350°F.

Brown beef in large skillet over medium heat about 10 minutes; drain off fat.

Add bell peppers and onion; cook and stir until tender, about 4 minutes. Stir in potatoes, tomato sauce, water, tomato paste, salt, basil and black pepper.

Spoon half of mixture into 13×9×2-inch baking pan or 3-quart baking dish; top with half of cheese. Spoon remaining meat mixture evenly over cheese. Cover pan with aluminum foil. Bake 45 minutes.

Cut remaining cheese into decorative shapes; place on top of casserole. Let stand loosely covered until cheese melts, about 5 minutes. *Makes 8 to 10 servings*

Patchwork Casserole

Chili Spaghetti Casserole

8 ounces uncooked
  spaghetti

1 pound lean ground beef

1 medium onion, chopped

¼ teaspoon salt

⅛ teaspoon black pepper

1 can (15 ounces)
  vegetarian chili with
  beans

1 can (14½ ounces)
  Italian-style stewed
  tomatoes, undrained

1½ cups (6 ounces)
  shredded sharp
  Cheddar cheese,
  divided

½ cup reduced-fat sour
  cream

1½ teaspoons chili powder

¼ teaspoon garlic powder

Preheat oven to 350°F. Spray 13×9-inch baking dish with nonstick cooking spray.

Cook pasta according to package directions until al dente. Drain and place in prepared dish.

Meanwhile, place beef and onion in large skillet; season with salt and pepper. Brown beef over medium-high heat until beef is no longer pink, stirring to separate meat; drain fat. Stir in chili, tomatoes with juice, 1 cup cheese, sour cream, chili powder and garlic powder.

Add chili mixture to pasta; stir until pasta is well coated. Sprinkle with remaining ½ cup cheese.

Cover tightly with foil and bake 30 minutes or until hot and bubbly. Let stand 5 minutes before serving.

Makes 8 servings

Magical Tip

The next time you're making a casserole, assemble and bake two. Allow one to cool completely, then wrap it in heavy-duty foil and freeze it for another day. To reheat a frozen 2-quart casserole, unwrap it and microwave, covered, at HIGH for 20 to 30 minutes, stirring once or twice during cooking. Allow to stand about 5 minutes.

Chili Spaghetti Casserole

Spinach Lasagna

1 pound ground beef

¼ pound fresh mushrooms, thinly sliced

1 medium onion, chopped

1 clove garlic, minced

1 can (28 ounces) Italian plum tomatoes, undrained

1¼ teaspoons salt, divided

¾ teaspoon dried oregano leaves, crushed

¾ teaspoon dried basil leaves, crushed

¼ teaspoon black pepper, divided

9 uncooked lasagna noodles

¼ cup plus 1 tablespoon butter or margarine, divided

¼ cup all-purpose flour

⅛ teaspoon ground nutmeg

2 cups milk

1½ cups shredded mozzarella cheese (about 6 ounces), divided

½ cup freshly grated Parmesan cheese, divided

1 package (10 ounces) frozen chopped spinach, thawed and squeezed dry

1. For meat sauce, crumble ground beef into large skillet over medium-high heat. Brown 8 to 10 minutes, stirring to separate meat, until meat loses its pink color. Stir in mushrooms, onion and garlic; cook over medium heat 5 minutes or until onion is tender.

2. Press tomatoes with juice through sieve into meat mixture; discard seeds. Stir in ¾ teaspoon salt, oregano, basil and ⅛ teaspoon pepper. Bring to a boil over medium-high heat; reduce heat to low. Cover and simmer 40 minutes, stirring occasionally. Uncover and simmer 15 to 20 minutes more until sauce thickens. Set aside.

3. Add lasagna noodles to large pot of boiling salted water, 1 at a time, allowing noodles to soften and fit into pot. Cook 10 minutes or just until al dente. Drain noodles; rinse with cold water. Drain again; hang individually over pot rim to prevent sticking. Set aside.

4. For cheese sauce, melt ¼ cup butter in medium saucepan over medium heat. Stir in flour, remaining ½ teaspoon salt, remaining ⅛ teaspoon pepper and nutmeg; cook and stir until bubbly. Whisk in milk; cook and stir until sauce thickens and bubbles. Cook and stir 1 minute more. Remove from heat. Stir in 1 cup mozzarella and ¼ cup Parmesan cheese. Stir until smooth. Set aside.

5. Preheat oven to 350°F. Spread remaining 1 tablespoon butter on bottom and sides of 12×8-inch baking dish with waxed paper. Spread noodles in single layer on clean kitchen (not paper) towel. Pat noodles dry.

Continued on page 122

Spinach Lasagna

120

Spinach Lasagna, continued from page 120

6. Arrange 3 lasagna noodles in single layer, overlapping slightly, in bottom of baking dish. Top with ½ of reserved meat sauce; spread evenly. Spread ½ of reserved cheese sauce over meat sauce in even layer.

7. Repeat layers once, using 3 noodles, remaining meat sauce and remaining cheese sauce. Sprinkle spinach over cheese sauce in even layer; pat down lightly. Arrange remaining 3 lasagna noodles over spinach.

8. Mix remaining ½ cup mozzarella and ¼ cup Parmesan cheese in cup. Sprinkle cheeses evenly over top of lasagna to completely cover lasagna noodles. Bake 40 minutes or until top is golden and edges are bubbly. Let lasagna stand 10 minutes before serving. Garnish as desired. *Makes 6 servings*

Zucchini Pasta Bake

1 ½ **cups uncooked pasta tubes**
½ **pound ground beef**
½ **cup chopped onion**
1 **clove garlic, minced**
Salt and pepper
1 **can (14 ½ ounces) DEL MONTE® Zucchini with Italian-Style Tomato Sauce**
1 **teaspoon dried basil, crushed**
1 **cup (4 ounces) shredded Monterey Jack cheese**

1. Cook pasta according to package directions; drain.

2. Cook beef with onion and garlic in large skillet; drain. Season with salt and pepper.

3. Stir in zucchini with tomato sauce and basil. Place pasta in 8-inch square baking dish. Top with meat mixture.

4. Bake at 350°F for 15 minutes. Top with cheese. Bake 3 minutes or until cheese is melted.

Makes 4 servings

Prep and Cook Time: 33 minutes

Johnnie Marzetti

1 tablespoon CRISCO® Oil*
1 cup chopped celery
1 cup chopped onion
1 medium green bell
   pepper, chopped
1 pound ground beef
1 can (14½ ounces)
   Italian-style stewed
   tomatoes
1 can (8 ounces) tomato
   sauce
1 can (6 ounces) tomato
   paste
1 cup water
1 bay leaf
1½ teaspoons dried basil
   leaves
1¼ teaspoons salt
¼ teaspoon black pepper
1 package (12 ounces) egg
   noodles, cooked and
   well drained
½ cup plain dry bread
   crumbs
1 cup (4 ounces) shredded
   sharp Cheddar cheese

*Use your favorite Crisco Oil product.

1. Heat oven to 375°F. Oil 12½×8½×2-inch baking dish lightly. Place cooling rack on countertop.

2. Heat one tablespoon oil in large skillet on medium heat. Add celery, onion and green pepper. Cook and stir until tender. Remove vegetables from skillet. Set aside. Add meat to skillet. Cook until browned, stirring occasionally. Return vegetables to skillet. Add tomatoes, tomato sauce, tomato paste, water, bay leaf, basil, salt and black pepper. Reduce heat to low. Simmer 5 minutes, stirring occasionally. Remove bay leaf.

3. Place noodles in baking dish. Spoon meat mixture over noodles. Sprinkle with bread crumbs and cheese.

4. Bake at 375°F for 15 to 20 minutes or until cheese melts. *Do not overbake.* Remove baking dish to cooling rack. Garnish, if desired.   *Makes 8 servings*

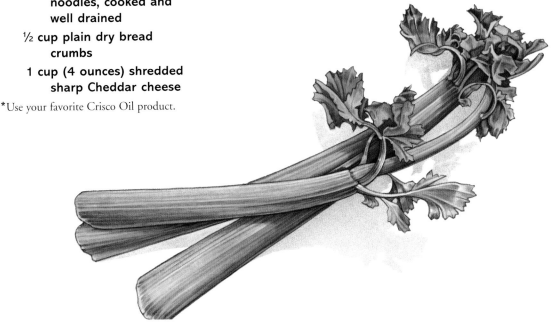

Skillets

Chuckwagon BBQ Rice Round-Up

1 pound lean ground beef
1 (6.8-ounce) package RICE-A-RONI® Beef Flavor
2 tablespoons margarine or butter
2 cups frozen corn
½ cup prepared barbecue sauce
½ cup (2 ounces) shredded Cheddar cheese

1. In large skillet over medium-high heat, brown ground beef until well cooked. Remove from skillet; drain. Set aside.

2. In same skillet over medium heat, sauté rice-vermicelli mix with margarine until vermicelli is golden brown.

3. Slowly stir in 2½ cups water, corn and Special Seasonings; bring to a boil. Reduce heat to low. Cover; simmer 15 to 20 minutes or until rice is tender.

4. Stir in barbecue sauce and ground beef. Sprinkle with cheese. Cover; let stand 3 to 5 minutes or until cheese is melted. *Makes 4 servings*

Tip: Salsa can be substituted for barbecue sauce.

Prep Time: 5 minutes
Cook Time: 25 minutes

Chuckwagon BBQ Rice Round-Up

Italian Beef Burrito

1½ pounds ground beef

2 medium onions, finely chopped

2 medium red and/or green bell peppers, chopped

1 jar (26 to 28 ounces) RAGÚ® Robusto!™ Pasta Sauce

½ teaspoon dried oregano leaves, crushed

8 (10-inch) flour tortillas, warmed

2 cups shredded mozzarella cheese (about 8 ounces)

1. In 12-inch skillet, brown ground beef over medium-high heat.

2. Stir in onions and red bell peppers and cook, stirring occasionally, 5 minutes or until tender; drain. Stir in Ragú Pasta Sauce and oregano; heat through.

3. To serve, top each tortilla with ¼ cup cheese and 1 cup ground beef mixture; roll up and serve.

Makes 8 servings

Prep Time: 15 minutes
Cook Time: 15 minutes

Southwestern Skillet Dinner

1 pound ground beef

2 teaspoons chili powder

1 jar (16 ounces) thick and chunky salsa

1½ cups BIRDS EYE® frozen Corn

¾ cup shredded Cheddar cheese

• Cook ground beef in large skillet over high heat until well browned, about 8 minutes; drain. Stir in chili powder; cook 1 minute.

• Add salsa and corn; bring to boil. Reduce heat to medium; cover and cook 4 minutes.

• Sprinkle with cheese; cover and cook until cheese melts.

Makes about 4 servings

Serving Suggestion: Serve with rice or tortilla chips. Or, serve as a taco filling.

Prep Time: 5 minutes
Cook Time: 20 minutes

Italian Beef Burrito

Velveeta® Cheeseburger Mac

Serious **Skillets**

1 pound ground beef
2¾ cups water
⅓ cup catsup
1 to 2 teaspoons onion powder
2 cups (8 ounces) elbow macaroni, uncooked
¾ pound (12 ounces) VELVEETA® Pasteurized Prepared Cheese Product, cut up

1. Brown meat in large skillet; drain.

2. Stir in water, catsup and onion powder. Bring to a boil. Stir in macaroni. Reduce heat to medium-low; cover. Simmer 8 to 10 minutes or until macaroni is tender.

3. Add Velveeta; stir until melted.

Makes 4 to 6 servings

Safe Food Handling: Store ground beef in the coldest part of the refrigerator for up to 2 days. Make sure raw juices do not touch other foods. Ground meat can be wrapped airtight and frozen for up to 3 months.

Prep Time: 10 minutes
Cook Time: 15 minutes

Skillet Italiano

1 pound ground beef
½ medium onion, chopped
1 package (1.5 ounces) LAWRY'S® Original-Style Spaghetti Sauce Spices & Seasonings
1 can (14½ ounces) whole tomatoes, cut up, undrained
1 package (10 ounces) frozen Italian-cut green beans, thawed
LAWRY'S® Seasoned Salt, to taste
1 cup (4 ounces) shredded cheddar cheese

In large skillet, cook ground beef and onion until beef is browned and crumbly; drain fat. Add Original-Style Spaghetti Sauce Spices & Seasonings, tomatoes with juice, and beans; mix well. Bring to a boil over medium-high heat; reduce heat to low, cover and simmer 20 minutes. Add Seasoned Salt to taste. Top with cheese; cover and heat until cheese melts.

Makes 4 to 6 servings

Serving Suggestion: Serve with warm bread and a tossed fruit salad.

Velveeta® Cheeseburger Mac

Campbell's® Country Skillet Supper

1 pound ground beef

1 medium onion, chopped (about ½ cup)

⅛ teaspoon garlic powder *or* 1 clove garlic, minced

1 can (10¾ ounces) CAMPBELL'S® Condensed Golden Mushroom Soup

1 can (10½ ounces) CAMPBELL'S® Condensed Beef Broth

1 can (14½ ounces) diced tomatoes

1 small zucchini, sliced (about 1 cup)

½ teaspoon dried thyme leaves, crushed

1½ cups *uncooked* corkscrew pasta

1. In medium skillet over medium-high heat, cook beef, onion and garlic powder until beef is browned, stirring to separate meat. Pour off fat.

2. Add soup, broth, tomatoes, zucchini and thyme. Heat to a boil. Stir in pasta. Reduce heat to low. Cook 15 minutes or until pasta is done, stirring often.

Makes 4 servings

Campbell's® Country Skillet Supper Provençal: Top with sliced pitted ripe olives.

Prep Time: 5 minutes
Cook Time: 25 minutes

Campbell's® Country Skillet Supper

Western Wagon Wheels

1 pound lean ground beef
   or ground turkey

2 cups wagon wheel pasta,
   uncooked

1 can (14½ ounces)
   stewed tomatoes

1½ cups water

1 box (10 ounces) BIRDS
   EYE® frozen Sweet
   Corn

½ cup barbecue sauce

   Salt and pepper to taste

• In large skillet, cook beef over medium heat 5 minutes or until well browned.

• Stir in pasta, tomatoes, water, corn and barbecue sauce; bring to boil.

• Reduce heat to low; cover and simmer 15 to 20 minutes or until pasta is tender, stirring occasionally. Season with salt and pepper.   *Makes 4 servings*

Serving Suggestion: Serve with corn bread or corn muffins.

Prep Time: 5 minutes
Cook Time: 25 minutes

Magical Tip

Pasta is favored by dieters and athletes alike. It is rich in energizing complex carbohydrates and essential B vitamins. Because complex carbohydrates are digested slowly they help to curb the appetite and sustain body energy. Low in fat and cholesterol, pasta is easy to prepare and goes with almost any meal. With the multitude of shapes, sizes and colors available, no wonder pasta is showing up on dinner tables everywhere.

Western Wagon Wheels

Pizza Olé

Serious Skillets

1 pound ground beef
1 (1-ounce) package taco
   seasoning
1 (30-ounce) can
   ROSARITA® Traditional
   Refried Beans
4 extra-large tortilla wraps
4 cups shredded Monterey
   Jack cheese
   Sliced green onion
   Diced fresh tomato
   Sliced black olives

In large nonstick skillet, cook beef and taco seasoning according to taco seasoning package directions. Add beans; mix well until heated through.

Spread half of bean mixture onto 1 tortilla. Top with 1 tortilla; sprinkle with 2 cups cheese. Repeat with remaining bean mixture, tortillas and cheese.

Place pizzas on baking sheet. Bake at 400°F for 10 minutes or until cheese is melted. Sprinkle pizzas with green onion, tomato and olives. Cut each pizza into 8 wedges. *Makes 16 servings*

Beef with Cabbage and Carrots

¾ pound extra-lean (90%
   lean) ground beef
4 cups shredded cabbage
1½ cups shredded carrot
   (1 large carrot)
½ teaspoon caraway seeds
2 tablespoons seasoned
   rice vinegar
   Salt and black pepper

Brown ground beef in large skillet; drain. Reduce heat to low. Stir in cabbage, carrot and caraway seeds; cover. Cook 10 minutes or until vegetables are tender, stirring occasionally. Stir in vinegar. (Add 1 tablespoon water for extra moistness, if desired.) Season with salt and pepper to taste. *Makes 4 servings*

Variation: Substitute 1 teaspoon sugar and 1 tablespoon white wine vinegar for 2 tablespoons seasoned rice vinegar.

Pizza Olé

Rapid Ragú® Chili

1½ **pounds lean ground beef**
1 **medium onion, chopped**
2 **tablespoons chili powder**
1 **can (19 ounces) red kidney beans, rinsed and drained**
1 **jar (26 to 28 ounces) RAGÚ® Old World Style® Pasta Sauce**
1 **cup shredded Cheddar cheese (about 4 ounces)**

1. In 12-inch skillet, brown ground beef with onion and chili powder over medium-high heat, stirring occasionally. Stir in beans and Ragú Pasta Sauce.

2. Bring to a boil over high heat. Reduce heat to low and simmer covered, stirring occasionally, 20 minutes. Top with cheese. Serve, if desired, over hot cooked rice.

Makes 6 servings

Prep Time: 10 minutes
Cook Time: 25 minutes

Rapid Ragú® Chili

Mexican Beef Stir-Fry

1 pound beef flank steak

2 tablespoons vegetable oil

1 teaspoon ground cumin

1 teaspoon dried oregano leaves

1 clove garlic, crushed

1 red or green bell pepper, cut into thin strips

1 medium onion, cut into thin wedges

1 to 2 jalapeño peppers,* thinly sliced

3 cups thinly sliced lettuce

*Jalapeño peppers can sting and irritate the skin; wear rubber gloves when handling peppers and do not touch eyes. Wash hands after handling. Remove interior ribs and seeds if a milder flavor is desired.

Cut beef steak into ⅛-inch-thick strips. Combine oil, cumin, oregano and garlic in small bowl. Heat ½ oil mixture in large nonstick skillet over medium-high heat. Add bell pepper, onion and jalapeño pepper; stir-fry 2 to 3 minutes or until crisp-tender. Remove and reserve. In same skillet, stir-fry beef strips (½ at a time) in remaining oil mixture 1 to 2 minutes. Return vegetables to skillet and heat through. Serve beef mixture over lettuce.   *Makes 4 servings*

Tip: Recipe may also be prepared using beef top sirloin or top round steak cut 1 inch thick.

Serving Suggestion: Serve with corn bread twists.

Favorite recipe from **North Dakota Beef Commission**

Beef Fried Rice

¾ pound extra-lean (90% lean) ground beef

6 green onions, chopped

3 large ribs celery, chopped

8 ounces bean sprouts

½ cup sliced fresh mushrooms

½ cup finely chopped red bell pepper

1 teaspoon grated fresh ginger

3 cups cooked rice

2 tablespoons soy sauce

Salt and black pepper

Brown ground beef in large skillet; drain. Stir in onions, celery, bean sprouts, mushrooms, red bell pepper and ginger. Cook over medium-high heat 5 minutes or until vegetables are crisp-tender, stirring frequently. Stir in rice and soy sauce. Season with salt and black pepper to taste. Heat through, stirring occasionally.

Makes 4 servings

Mexican Beef Stir-Fry

Velveeta® Cheesy Beef Stroganoff

Serious **Skillets**

1 pound ground beef

2 cups water

3 cups (6 ounces) medium egg noodles, uncooked

¾ pound (12 ounces) VELVEETA® Pasteurized Prepared Cheese Product, cut up

1 can (10¾ ounces) condensed cream of mushroom soup

¼ teaspoon black pepper

1. Brown meat in large skillet; drain.

2. Stir in water. Bring to boil. Stir in noodles. Reduce heat to medium-low; cover. Simmer 8 minutes or until noodles are tender.

3. Add Velveeta, soup and pepper; stir until Velveeta is melted.   *Makes 4 to 6 servings*

Prep Time: 10 minutes
Cook Time: 15 minutes

Velveeta® Cheesy Tacos

1 pound ground beef

¼ cup water

1 package (1 ¼ ounces) TACO BELL® HOME ORIGINALS®* Taco Seasoning Mix

¾ pound (12 ounces) VELVEETA® Mexican Pasteurized Process Cheese Spread with Jalapeño Peppers, cut up

1 package (4.5 ounces) TACO BELL® HOME ORIGINALS®* Taco Shells *or* 12 flour tortillas (8 inch)

*TACO BELL and HOME ORIGINALS are registered trademarks owned and licensed by Taco Bell Corp.

1. Brown meat in large skillet; drain. Stir in water and taco seasoning mix.

2. Add Velveeta; stir on low heat until Velveeta is melted.

3. Fill heated taco shells with meat mixture. Top with your favorite toppings, such as shredded lettuce, chopped tomato and Taco Bell Home Originals Thick 'N Chunky Salsa.   *Makes 4 to 6 servings*

Serving Suggestion: Cheesy Tacos are a fun family dinner. Have your child place your family's favorite taco toppings, such as shredded lettuce and chopped tomato, in a muffin tin to pass around at the table.

Prep Time: 5 minutes
Cook Time: 15 minutes

Velveeta® Cheesy Beef Stroganoff

Zesty Mexican Stir-Fry Fajitas

1 pound beef sirloin, flank or round steak, thinly sliced

1 large red bell pepper, thinly sliced

1 medium onion, sliced

1 jar (12 ounces) prepared beef gravy

2 tablespoons *Frank's®* *RedHot®* Cayenne Pepper Sauce

1 teaspoon garlic powder

1 teaspoon dried oregano leaves

1 teaspoon ground cumin

8 flour tortillas, heated

1. Heat *2 tablespoons oil* in large skillet over high heat until hot. Stir-fry beef in batches 5 minutes or until browned.

2. Add pepper and onion; cook 2 minutes. Add remaining ingredients. Stir-fry an additional 2 minutes. Spoon mixture onto tortillas; roll up. Splash on more ***Frank's RedHot*** Sauce to taste. *Makes 4 servings*

Prep Time: 10 minutes
Cook Time: 10 minutes

Zesty Mexican Stir-Fry Fajitas

Campbell's® Easy Skillet Beef & Hash Browns

1 pound ground beef

1 can (10¾ ounces)
CAMPBELL'S®
Condensed Cream of
Celery Soup *or* 98%
Fat Free Cream of
Celery Soup

½ cup water

¼ cup ketchup

1 tablespoon
Worcestershire sauce

2 cups frozen diced
potatoes (hash browns)

3 slices process American
cheese (about
3 ounces)

1. In medium skillet over medium-high heat, cook beef until browned, stirring to separate meat. Pour off fat.

2. Add soup, water, ketchup and Worcestershire. Heat to a boil. Stir in potatoes. Reduce heat to medium-low. Cover and cook 10 minutes or until potatoes are done, stirring occasionally. Top with cheese.

Makes 4 servings

Prep/Cook Time: 20 minutes

Campbell's® Quick Beef Skillet

1 pound ground beef

1 can (10¾ ounces)
CAMPBELL'S®
Condensed Tomato
Soup

¼ cup water

1 tablespoon
Worcestershire sauce

¼ teaspoon pepper

1 can (about 15 ounces)
sliced potatoes,
drained

1 can (about 8 ounces)
sliced carrots, drained

1. In medium skillet over medium-high heat, cook beef until browned, stirring to separate meat. Pour off fat.

2. Add soup, water, Worcestershire, pepper, potatoes and carrots. Reduce heat to low and heat through.

Makes 4 servings

Prep/Cook Time: 15 minutes

*Bottom to top: Campbell's® Easy Skillet Beef
& Hash Browns, Campbell's® Quick Beef Skillet*

Tijuana Tacos

1 teaspoon vegetable oil

½ cup chopped green bell pepper

½ cup chopped green onions

1 jalapeño pepper,* minced

1 pound lean ground beef

1 cup salsa

½ teaspoon ground cumin

½ teaspoon chili powder

8 taco shells

2 cups shredded lettuce

2 cups chopped tomatoes

1½ cups (6 ounces) shredded Cheddar cheese

*Jalapeño peppers can sting and irritate the skin; wear rubber gloves when handling peppers and do not touch eyes. Wash hands after handling.

Heat oil in large nonstick skillet over medium-high heat until hot. Add bell pepper, onions and jalapeño pepper; cook and stir 5 minutes or until vegetables are tender.

Add beef to vegetable mixture. Cook until no longer pink; pour off excess fat. Add salsa, cumin and chili powder to meat mixture; stir to combine.

Spoon beef mixture into taco shells. Top with lettuce, tomatoes and Cheddar cheese. Garnish as desired.

Makes 8 servings

Tijuana Tacos

Velveeta® Salsa Mac

1 pound ground beef

1 jar (16 ounces) TACO
   BELL® HOME
   ORIGINALS®* Thick 'N
   Chunky Salsa

1¾ cups water

2 cups (8 ounces) elbow
   macaroni, uncooked

¾ pound (12 ounces)
   VELVEETA® Pasteurized
   Prepared Cheese
   Product, cut up

*TACO BELL and HOME
ORIGINALS are registered trademarks
owned and licensed by Taco Bell Corp.

1. Brown meat in large skillet; drain.

2. Stir in salsa and water. Bring to a boil. Stir in macaroni. Reduce heat to medium-low; cover. Simmer 8 to 10 minutes or until macaroni is tender.

3. Add Velveeta; stir until melted.

Makes 4 to 6 servings

Spicy Substitute: For an extra spicy kick in Salsa Mac, try making it with Velveeta Mild or Hot Mexican Pasteurized Process Cheese Spread with Jalapeño Peppers. Be careful though...the hot is really hot!

Prep Time: 10 minutes
Cook Time: 15 minutes

Velveeta® Salsa Mac

Beefy Bean Skillet

1 box (9 ounces) BIRDS
    EYE® frozen Cut Green
    Beans
½ pound lean ground beef
½ cup chopped onion
1 cup instant rice
1 can (10 ounces) au jus
    gravy*
¾ cup ketchup

*Or, substitute 1 can (10 ounces) beef
broth.

• In medium saucepan, cook green beans according to package directions; drain and set aside.

• Meanwhile, in large skillet, brown beef; drain excess fat. Add onion; cook and stir until onion is tender.

• Add rice, gravy and ketchup. Bring to boil over medium-high heat; cover and reduce heat to medium-low. Simmer 5 to 10 minutes or until rice is cooked, stirring occasionally.

• Stir in beans. Simmer until heated through.

Makes 4 servings

Prep Time: 10 minutes
Cook Time: 20 minutes

Beefy Bean Skillet

Little Italy Skillet Meal (Greek Island Skillet)

¾ **pound lean ground beef**

3 cups water

1 can (14 ounces) diced tomatoes, undrained

1 package KNORR® Recipe Classics™ Roasted Garlic Soup, Dip and Recipe Mix

2½ **cups (8 ounces) uncooked pasta twists**

1 package (10 ounces) frozen chopped spinach, thawed and drained

1 can (2.2 ounces) sliced ripe olives, drained (about ½ cup)

¼ **cup crumbled feta cheese or grated Parmesan cheese (optional)**

• In large skillet, sauté ground beef over medium-high heat 5 minutes or until lightly browned. Spoon off excess drippings. Add water, tomatoes with juice and recipe mix; bring to a boil.

• Stir in pasta and return to boiling; reduce heat, cover and simmer 8 to 10 minutes or until pasta is tender, stirring frequently.

• Stir in spinach and olives. Simmer 2 minutes or until heated through. If desired, sprinkle with cheese.

Makes 4 servings

Prep Time: 25 to 30 minutes

Creamy Beef and Carrot Topped Baked Potatoes

1 tablespoon CRISCO® Oil*

1 cup shredded carrot

½ **cup chopped onion**

1 pound ground beef round

1 teaspoon salt

Dash of pepper

¼ **cup all-purpose flour**

2 cups beef broth

1 teaspoon Worcestershire sauce

6 hot baked medium potatoes

1. Heat oil in large skillet on medium heat. Add carrot and onion. Cook and stir until tender. Add beef, salt and pepper. Cook until meat is browned, stirring occasionally; drain. Sprinkle flour over meat mixture. Stir until blended.

2. Add broth and Worcestershire sauce to skillet. Cook and stir until thickened.

3. Place baked potatoes on serving plate. Split. Push ends toward center to open. Spoon about ½ cup meat mixture into each potato. Garnish, if desired.

Makes 6 servings

*Use your favorite Crisco Oil product.

Nifty Nacho Dinner

8 ounces lean ground beef

1 (6.8-ounce) package RICE-A-RONI® Beef Flavor

2 tablespoons margarine or butter

1 (16-ounce) can refried beans

1 (11-ounce) can Mexican-style corn or sweet corn, drained

1½ cups (6 ounces) shredded Cheddar cheese, divided

Tortilla chips

1. In large skillet over medium-high heat, brown ground beef. Remove from skillet; drain. Set aside.

2. In same skillet over medium heat, sauté rice-vermicelli mix with margarine until vermicelli is golden brown.

3. Slowly stir in 2½ cups water and Special Seasonings; bring to a boil. Reduce heat to low. Cover; simmer 10 minutes.

4. Stir in refried beans, corn, 1 cup cheese and beef; return to a simmer. Cover; simmer 5 to 10 minutes or until rice is tender. Top with remaining ½ cup cheese. Serve in skillet with tortilla chips.   *Makes 6 servings*

Prep Time: 5 minutes
Cook Time: 30 minutes

serious **Skillets**

Skillet Spaghetti and Sausage

¼ pound mild or hot Italian sausage links, sliced

½ pound ground beef

¼ teaspoon dried oregano, crushed

4 ounces spaghetti, broken in half

1 can (14½ ounces) DEL MONTE® Diced Tomatoes with Basil, Garlic & Oregano

1 can (8 ounces) DEL MONTE Tomato Sauce

1½ cups sliced fresh mushrooms

2 stalks celery, sliced

1. Brown sausage in large skillet over medium-high heat. Add beef and oregano; season to taste with salt and pepper, if desired.

2. Cook, stirring occasionally, until beef is browned; drain.

3. Add pasta, 1 cup water, undrained tomatoes, tomato sauce, mushrooms and celery. Bring to a boil, stirring occasionally.

4. Reduce heat; cover and simmer 12 to 14 minutes or until spaghetti is tender. Garnish with grated Parmesan cheese and chopped parsley, if desired. Serve immediately.
Makes 4 to 6 servings

Prep Time: 5 minutes
Cook Time: 30 minutes

Acknowledgments

The publisher would like to thank the companies and organizations listed below for the use of their recipes and photographs in this publication.

A.1.® Steak Sauce

Birds Eye®

Campbell Soup Company

ConAgra Grocery Products Company

Del Monte Corporation

Grey Poupon® Dijon Mustard

Heinz U.S.A.

Holland House® is a registered trademark of Mott's, Inc.

Kikkoman International Inc.

The Kingsford Products Company

Kraft Foods Holdings

Lawry's® Foods, Inc.

National Onion Association

National Turkey Federation

Nestlé USA

North Dakota Beef Commission

Perdue Farms Incorporated

Reckitt Benckiser

The J.M. Smucker Company

The Golden Grain Company®

Unilever Bestfoods North America

Wisconsin Milk Marketing Board

Acknowledgments

Index

Index

METRIC CONVERSION CHART

VOLUME MEASUREMENTS (dry)

1/8 teaspoon = 0.5 mL
1/4 teaspoon = 1 mL
1/2 teaspoon = 2 mL
3/4 teaspoon = 4 mL
1 teaspoon = 5 mL
1 tablespoon = 15 mL
2 tablespoons = 30 mL
1/4 cup = 60 mL
1/3 cup = 75 mL
1/2 cup = 125 mL
2/3 cup = 150 mL
3/4 cup = 175 mL
1 cup = 250 mL
2 cups = 1 pint = 500 mL
3 cups = 750 mL
4 cups = 1 quart = 1 L

VOLUME MEASUREMENTS (fluid)

1 fluid ounce (2 tablespoons) = 30 mL
4 fluid ounces (1/2 cup) = 125 mL
8 fluid ounces (1 cup) = 250 mL
12 fluid ounces (1 1/2 cups) = 375 mL
16 fluid ounces (2 cups) = 500 mL

WEIGHTS (mass)

1/2 ounce = 15 g
1 ounce = 30 g
3 ounces = 90 g
4 ounces = 120 g
8 ounces = 225 g
10 ounces = 285 g
12 ounces = 360 g
16 ounces = 1 pound = 450 g

DIMENSIONS

1/16 inch = 2 mm
1/8 inch = 3 mm
1/4 inch = 6 mm
1/2 inch = 1.5 cm
3/4 inch = 2 cm
1 inch = 2.5 cm

OVEN TEMPERATURES

250°F = 120°C
275°F = 140°C
300°F = 150°C
325°F = 160°C
350°F = 180°C
375°F = 190°C
400°F = 200°C
425°F = 220°C
450°F = 230°C

BAKING PAN SIZES

Utensil	Size in Inches/Quarts	Metric Volume	Size in Centimeters
Baking or Cake Pan (square or rectangular)	8×8×2	2 L	20×20×5
	9×9×2	2.5 L	23×23×5
	12×8×2	3 L	30×20×5
	13×9×2	3.5 L	33×23×5
Loaf Pan	8×4×3	1.5 L	20×10×7
	9×5×3	2 L	23×13×7
Round Layer Cake Pan	8×1½	1.2 L	20×4
	9×1½	1.5 L	23×4
Pie Plate	8×1¼	750 mL	20×3
	9×1¼	1 L	23×3
Baking Dish or Casserole	1 quart	1 L	—
	1½ quart	1.5 L	—
	2 quart	2 L	—